Seeking and Keeping Your Customers

SEEKING AND KEEPING YOUR CUSTOMERS

A Harvard Business Review Paperback

Harvard Business Review paperback No. 90063

ISBN 0-87584-279-8

The *Harvard Business Review* articles in this collection are
available as individual reprints. Discounts apply to quantity
purchases. For information and ordering contact Operations
Department, Harvard Business School Publishing Division,
Boston, MA 02163. Telephone: (617) 495-6192, 9 a.m. to 5
p.m. ET, Monday through Friday. Fax: (617) 495-6985, 24
hours a day.

Editor's Note: Some articles in this book may have been written before authors and editors began to take into consideration the role of women in management. We hope the archaic
usage representing all managers as male does not detract from
the usefulness of the collection.

Printed in the United States of America by Harvard
University, Office of the University Publisher.
93 92 91   5 4 3 2 1

Contents

Thinking Strategically about Customers

Manage Customers for Profits (Not Just Sales)
Benson P. Shapiro, V. Kasturi Rangan, Rowland T. Moriarty, and Elliot B. Ross
3

It costs more to fill some customers' orders than others. Do your prices reflect the differences?

Porsche on Nichemanship
David E. Gumpert
11

Insights from Porsche executives Peter Schutz and Jack Cook on how to tailor a product to appeal to a special class of customers.

Competing on the Eight Dimensions of Quality
David A. Garvin
21

Quality means more than simply protecting customers from annoyances. By creating products that reflect customers' needs and preferences, companies gain a competitive advantage.

Reaching and Cultivating Customers

Build Customer Relationships That Last
Barbara Bund Jackson
33

How close can industrial marketers get to their customers—and for how long? Successful relationship marketing involves doing a large number of things right, consistently, over time.

Humanize Your Selling Strategy
Harvey B. Mackay
43

At Mackay Envelope Corporation, "know your customer" isn't a cliché, it's the foundation of the business.

Negotiating with a Customer You Can't Afford to Lose
Thomas C. Keiser
51

When your customer turns into Attila the Hun, will you still be able to close the sale?

Customer-Driven Distribution Systems
Louis W. Stern and Frederick D. Sturdivant
55

Marketing executives often underestimate the importance of distribution systems. By studying what services and conveniences customers value, companies can design a distribution system that really performs.

Ensuring Customer Satisfaction

After the Sale Is Over ...
Theodore Levitt
63

As the economy becomes more service and technology oriented, the seller's focus will need to shift from simply landing sales to ensuring buyer satisfaction after the purchase.

The Case of the Complaining Customer
Dan Finkelman and Tony Goland
71

How much service does a company or store owe a customer? Is the customer always right? A case study examines the options faced by the president of Presto Cleaner when he received an angry letter from a customer.

The Power of Unconditional Service Guarantees
Christopher W.L. Hart
81

No-quibble guarantees are self-fulfilling—they promise quality and produce it.

My Employees Are My Service Guarantee
Timothy W. Firnstahl
91

A restaurant owner argues that the best way to satisfy an angry customer is to make immediate amends—by giving employees the obligation and authority to honor guarantees on their own.

Good Product Support Is Smart Marketing
Milind M. Lele and Uday S. Karmarkar
96

A variety of strategies, like equipment loans during downtimes and fast service response, is necessary to win and keep customers.

Thinking Strategically about Customers

Manage customers for profits (not just sales)

Benson P. Shapiro,
V. Kasturi Rangan,
Rowland T. Moriarty,
and Elliot B. Ross

High sales volume does not necessarily mean high income, as many companies have found to their sorrow. In fact, profits (as a percentage of sales) are often much higher on some orders than on others, for reasons managers sometimes do not well understand. If prices are appropriate, why is there such striking variation? Let's look at two examples of selling and pricing anomalies:

☐ A plumbing fixtures manufacturer raised prices to discourage the "worthless" small custom orders that were disrupting the factory. But a series of price hikes failed to reduce unit sales volume. A study of operations two years later revealed that the most profitable orders were these custom orders. The new high prices more than compensated for costs; customers weren't changing suppliers because of high switching expenses; and competitors had shied from short runs because of the conventional wisdom in the industry.

☐ A prominent producer of capital equipment, realizing it was losing big sales potential in its largest accounts, started a national account program. It included heavy sales support with experienced account managers; participation by high-level executives; special support like applications engineering, custom design services, unusual maintenance work, and expedited delivery; and a national purchase agreement with a hefty graduated volume discount.

Customers, however, viewed the program as merely a dog-and-pony show, having no sub-

Benson Shapiro, Kasturi Rangan, and Rowland Moriarty are professor, assistant professor, and associate professor of business administration, respectively, at the Harvard Business School. All teach marketing. Elliot Ross is a principal in the Cleveland office of McKinsey & Company. He focuses on strategy formulation with industrial clients.

stance. To convince the skeptics, top executives personally offered greater sales and service support and even more generous discounts.

Sales finally turned upward, and this "success" justified even higher levels of support. But profit margins soon began to erode; the big national accounts, the company discovered, were generating losses that were large enough to offset the rise in volume and the profitability of smaller, allegedly less attractive accounts.

It costs more to fill some orders than others. Do your prices reflect the differences?

Clearly these two companies discovered that it costs more to fill some orders than others. The plumbing fixtures executives raised prices precisely because they knew it was costing them more to fill small custom orders. The capital equipment company willingly took on extra costs in the hope of winning more sales. Management in both companies recognized that their price tags would vary, the first from boosted prices on custom orders, the other because of volume discounts. But executives in both companies failed to see that the cost and price variations would cause profound differences in the profitability of individual accounts and orders.

Many companies make this mistake. Managers pay little attention to account profitability, selection, and management. They seldom consider the magnitude, origins, and managerial implications of profit dispersion. In this article, we examine three central aspects of this important factor:

Costs to suppliers
Customer behavior
Management of customers

Costs to suppliers

Profit, of course, is the difference between the net price and the actual cost to serve. In terms of individual accounts and orders, there can be dramatic differences in both price and cost.

Despite legal constraints that encourage uniformity in pricing, notably the Robinson-Patman Act, customers usually pay quite different prices in practice. Some buyers can negotiate or take advantage of differential discounts because of their size or the functions they can perform themselves, like in-house maintenance or technical support. And some customers exploit deals and promotions more than others. Moreover, the costs of serving customers and filling orders can vary significantly.

Presale costs vary greatly from order to order and account to account. Geography matters: some customers and prospects are located far from the salesperson's home base or normal route. Some customers require seemingly endless sales calls, while others place their orders over the telephone. Some must be courted with top-level executives backed up by sophisticated account management techniques, while others need little special effort. Such variations in cost reflect differences in customers' buying processes or the nature of their buying teams. (Some teams are large and geographically and functionally dispersed; others are small and concentrated by location and/or function.) Finally, some customers demand intensive presale service, like applications engineering and custom design support, while others accept standard designs.

Production costs also vary by customer and by order. Order size influences cost, as do setup time, scrap rate, custom designs, special features and functions, unusual packaging, and even order timing. Off-peak orders cost less than those made when demand is heavy. Fast delivery costs more. Some orders call on more resources than others. A company that inventories products in anticipation of orders, however, will have difficulty tracing production costs to particular orders and customers. Accounting policies and conventions, furthermore, often cloud the distinctions in product costs.

Distribution costs naturally vary with the customer's location. It also costs more to ship via a preferred transportation mode, to drop ship to a separate receiving location, to find no back-haul opportunity, or to extend special logistics support like a field inventory.

Postsale service costs also differ. Sometimes customer training, installation, technical support, and repair and maintenance are profit-making operations, but businesses often bundle such services into the product price and the buyer pays "nothing extra" for them. For some items, including capital equipment, postsale costs are heavy.

Thus there are variations among customers in each of the four components of cost: before-the-sale expenses, production, distribution, and after-the-sale service. Moreover, if prices and costs do not correlate, the distribution of gross income will have a dispersion that is the sum of the individual price and cost dispersions, and thus much greater than either. Of course, prices and costs are often viewed as correlated, but our research suggests that they usually aren't— which produces a broad dispersion of account profitability.

Customers fall into four segments. Target your products to fit the most profitable groups.

With real cost-plus pricing, profitability could be uniform across customers despite wide variations in both costs and prices. But there is evidence that prices seldom reflect the actual costs in serving customers (though they may be somewhat related to production costs). In many businesses, the difference between the highest and lowest prices realized in similar transactions for the same product is as much as 30%, not including quantity discounts.[1] Look, for example, at the relationship between prices and total costs in one month's orders for a manufacturer of pipe resin (see *Exhibit I*). The diagonal line indicates a price level equal to costs. If gross margin were the same on all orders, the orders would all lie along a line parallel to the diagonal line. Instead, they are widely dispersed. Nearly 13% of sales volume resulted in losses of about a nickel a pound, while about 4% of volume generated an eight-cent profit. The rest fell somewhere between.

This pattern is not unusual. In a wide variety of situations, we have consistently observed a lack of correlation between price and the cost to serve.

1 See Elliot B. Ross,
"Making Money with Proactive Pricing,"
HBR November-December 1984, p. 145.

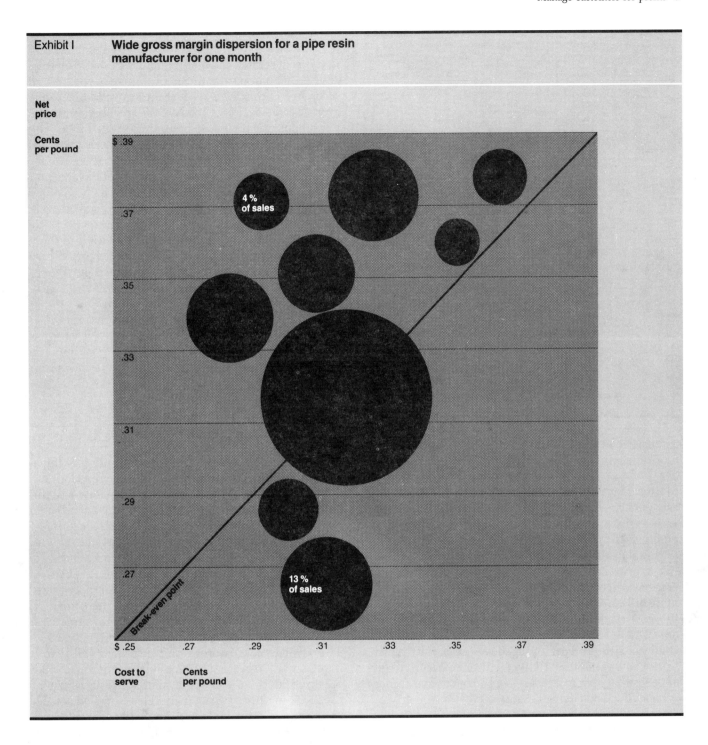

Exhibit I   **Wide gross margin dispersion for a pipe resin manufacturer for one month**

Net price

Cents per pound

$ .39

.37   4 % of sales

.35

.33

.31

.29

.27   13 % of sales

$ .25   .27   .29   .31   .33   .35   .37   .39

Break-even point

Cost to serve

Cents per pound

Some orders and customers generate losses, and in general the dispersion of profitability is wide.

Customer behavior

It is useful to think of customers in terms of two dimensions: net price realized and cost to serve. To show graphically the dynamics of the interplay between seller and buyer, we have devised a simple matrix (see *Exhibit II*). The vertical axis is net price, low to high, and the horizontal axis is cost to serve, low to high. This categorization is useful for any marketer. The *carriage trade* costs a great deal to serve but is willing to pay top dollar. (This category would include the customers of our introductory example, who placed small orders for high-cost custom plumbing fixtures.) At the opposite extreme are *bargain basement* customers – sensitive to price and relatively

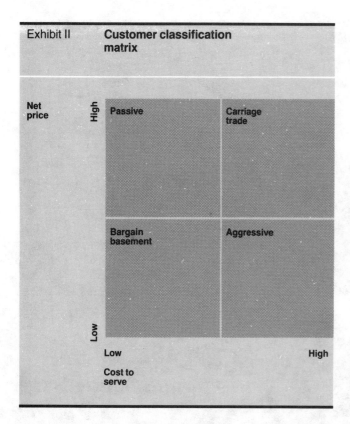

Exhibit II **Customer classification matrix**

Net price — High / Low

	Low ——— Cost to serve ——— High
High	Passive / Carriage trade
Low	Bargain basement / Aggressive

insensitive to service and quality. They can be served more cheaply than the carriage trade.

Serving *passive* customers costs less too, but they are willing to accept high prices. These accounts generate highly profitable orders. There are various reasons for their attitude. In some cases the product is too insignificant to warrant a tough negotiating stance over price. Other customers are insensitive to price because the product is crucial to their operation. Still others stay with their current supplier, more or less regardless of price, because of the prohibitive cost of switching. As an example from another industry, many major aircraft components cannot be changed without recertifying the entire aircraft. And in some cases vendor capability is so well matched to buyer needs that cost to serve is low though the customer is receiving (and paying for) fine service and quality.

Aggressive customers, on the other hand, demand (and often receive) the highest product quality, the best service, and low prices. Procter & Gamble, boasting an efficient procurement function, has a reputation among its suppliers for paying the least and getting the most. Aggressive buyers are usually powerful; their practice of buying in large quantities gives them leverage with suppliers in seeking price deals and more service. The national accounts described in the second example at the beginning of this article drove hard bargains with the capital equipment supplier.

Marketing managers often assume a strong correlation between net price and cost to serve; they reason that price-sensitive customers will accept

lower quality and service and demanding customers will pay more for better quality and service. Thinking in terms of service and quality demands unfortunately deflects attention from the critical issue of cost to serve. In addition, weak cost accounting practices that average costs over products, orders, and customers often support the high-cost, high-price myth. But as we have seen, costs and prices are not closely correlated.

A supplier of industrial packaging materials recently analyzed the profitability of its large national accounts. For each one it calculated approximate indicators of net price and cost to serve, based on averages of the aggregate values of a year's transactions. Top officers expected to find most of its customers in the carriage trade quadrant and the rest in the bargain basement. They were shocked when the results put about half of the 164 large customers in the passive and aggressive quadrants (see *Exhibit III*).

We believe this pattern is more common than is generally recognized. Among the various factors influencing buying behavior, the most important are the customer's situation and migration patterns.

Customer's situation

Four aspects of the customer's nature and position affect profitability: customer economics, power, the nature of the decision-making unit, and the institutional relationship between the buyer and seller.

As we all know, fundamental economics helps determine a buyer's price and service sensitivity. Customers are more sensitive to price when the product is a big part of their purchases, more sensitive to service when it has a big impact on their operations. Independent of economics, buying power, of course, is a major determinant of the buyer's ability to extract price concessions and service support from vendors. The power of big customers shows in their ability to handle many aspects of service support in-house – like breaking bulk – for which they demand price adjustments. Sometimes small customers also wield considerable power. A technological innovator that influences industry standards commands the eyes and ears of suppliers. Thus the relationship of cost to serve and customer size in this industry is not clear without careful measurement.

In respect to the decision-making unit, the purchase staff is generally sensitive to price, while engineering and production personnel are sensitive to service. These roles will affect decisions, depending on who most influences vendor choice and management.

Naturally, this element is bound up with any relationships that have built up between the buyer and seller. Long-standing friendships, long histories of satisfactory performance, and appreciation for

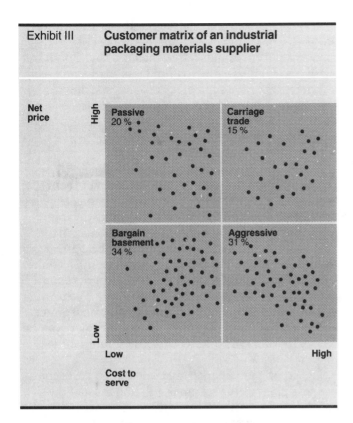

Exhibit III   **Customer matrix of an industrial packaging materials supplier**

Net price — High / Low

Passive
20 %

Carriage trade
15 %

Bargain basement
34 %

Aggressive
31 %

Cost to serve — Low / High

any special help or favors all tend to make customers reluctant to pressure suppliers for price and service concessions. Procter & Gamble rotates the responsibilities of its purchasing department members to discourage the development of strong personal relationships with vendors.

Migration patterns

Changes in organizational buying behavior and competitive activity can produce predictable patterns of change in customer profitability. Often a relationship begins in the carriage trade category. Customers need extensive sales and service support, insist on high product quality, and do not worry much about price if the product is new to them. They need the functionality and will pay for it.

Over time, however, as the customers gain experience with the product, they grow confident in dealing with the vendor and operating with less sales and service support or even without any. The cost of serving them is likely to decline, and they are likely to become more price sensitive. In addition, the buying influence of the customer's procurement department often grows, while the role of engineering and operating personnel diminishes. This shift of course reinforces the tendency toward price sensitivity and away from service concerns. Finally, through rival product offerings (often at lower prices), customers gain knowl-

edge that improves their competence with the product and thus their ability to demand price concessions and lessen their dependence on the vendor's support efforts.

If the customer perceives the product as trivial (as in the case of office supplies) and therefore does not seek it avidly, price sensitivity will not necessarily increase as service needs abate. In terms of the matrix of which *Exhibit II* is an example, migration will be toward the passive and bargain basement areas. If the buyer values the product and it is complex or service sensitive (like CAD/CAM equipment), the buyer may pressure the supplier for price reductions even while service requirements remain high. The migration tends to be downward from the carriage trade toward the aggressive quadrant, as in the case of electrical generation equipment for utilities. In commodities like pipe resin, a combination of customer experience, expanding influence of the purchasing staff, and increasing competitive imitation often leads customers into the bargain basement category.

Management of customers

The shifts toward the bargain basement and aggressive quadrants are part of the general tendency of products to evolve from high-margin specialties to low-margin commodities. The dispersion of customer profitability we have observed can be managed. We suggest a five-step action program: pinpoint your costs, know your profitability dispersion, focus your strategy, provide support systems, and analyze repeatedly.

Pinpoint your costs. Manufacturers can usually measure their factory costs better than costs incurred by the sales, applications engineering, logistics, and service functions. For instance, few companies have a sense of the cost of unscheduled executive effort to handle the demands of aggressive customers. So it seems likely that customer profitability varies more widely in businesses where a large percentage of the total expenditure is incurred outside the factory. This would be the case in many high-tech companies that have low manufacturing costs but spend a great deal on sales, design engineering, applications engineering, and systems integration.

Because many specialty products are custom designed and manufactured and carry heavy nonfactory costs, the cost dispersion for these products is greater than for commodities. But as we pointed out in our pipe resin example, profit dispersion can be high even in a commodity product.

Costs incurred at different times in the order cycle have different effects on the true cost to serve the customer or order. In major sales with long order cycles and long lead times, the presale effort may begin several years ahead, and service under warranty may extend several years after installation and billing. If the cost of capital is 15%, a dollar spent two years before the billing of the customer is worth $1.32, and a dollar spent three years after billing is worth only 61 cents at the time of delivery. Companies with long lead times and order cycles, such as sellers of power generation equipment and commercial airliners, with long-term, substantial service liabilities, evidently have cost dispersions much larger than average, except where progress payments balance out cost flows. These companies need particularly good control systems and management judgment to measure costs and act accordingly.

Without a good cost accounting system, says one manager, "It's management by anecdote."

Companies with poor cost accounting systems have no way to determine order, customer, product, or market segment profitability. Consequently, their cost control and management systems will be weak, and the result is likely to be above-average dispersion of costs. The sales manager of a large office equipment supplier who lacked adequate cost information described his situation thus: "It's management by anecdote. Salespeople regularly make passionate pleas for price relief on specific orders. When I press them for reasons, they say 'threat of competitive entry.' When I ask them if a cutback in service would be acceptable to make up for the price decrease, they give me a resounding no! What choice do you have in the absence of cost data, except to go by your judgment of the salesperson's credibility? I've wrongly accepted as many bad price relief requests as I've rejected."

An effective cost accounting system records data by product, order, and account, and records costs beyond the factory, including selling, transportation, applications or design engineering, and even unusual, unprogrammed activities like investments of blocks of corporate management time. Presale, production, distribution, and postsale service costs should all be recorded, analyzed, and related to orders and accounts.

Of course, there are enormous difficulties in creating and maintaining such a system. But even a system that estimates such costs only approximately can help a great deal. Twice a year, for example, one industrial company calculates the cost of serving three sizes of customers (large, medium, and small) and two sizes of orders (truckload and less-than-truckload) for a representative sample of accounts and orders. During the following six months, sales managers use these numbers to guide their decisions on price-relief requests.

Know your profitability dispersion. Once costs are known, the company can plot them against realized prices to show the dispersion of account profitability, as in *Exhibit II*. Clearly the framework must be adapted to the characteristics of the business. Similarly, the price axis should be defined in a meaningful way. Since list prices are often misleading, use some sort of net price. However, discounts should not be double-counted under costs as well. The ultimate objective is a measure of net profit by customer and order. Tracking cost and price data by order is an essential first step in building an account profitability matrix.

Companies that know their costs and use cost-plus pricing schemes will find most of their accounts in the bargain basement or carriage trade quadrants of the matrix. Though this pattern is perfectly reasonable, sales management should try to develop accounts in the passive quadrant. Many such customers will accept higher prices because they like the product so much. The cost to them of negotiating a lower price (or better service) outweighs the extra benefits they would get. The passive quadrant represents a region of maximum value for both the seller and the buyer.

A dispersion of profits is no bad thing; only not knowing it exists is. The best managed companies know their costs well and set prices on the basis of product value to customers rather than cost to serve. So they have some accounts in the passive categories. In fact, their profit dispersion will be greater than that of companies pricing on a cost-plus basis. The worst managed companies, ignorant of their costs and setting prices mainly in response to customer demands, are likely to have a large number of accounts in the aggressive category, with, obviously, pessimistic implications for profitability.

Focus your strategy. The next step is to use your knowledge of cost, price, and profit dispersion to define a strategy for managing your accounts. Here the company defines its personality. The low-cost, low-service, low-price provider would be in the lower left of a profitability matrix, while the company that offers differentiated and augmented products, intensive service, and customization—and, therefore, more value added—is in the upper right quadrant. Because any company's capability is necessarily limited, it cannot

span the entire dimension. If it tries to, the poor focus will leave the company vulnerable to competition. This will allow rivals to jump into the aggressive quadrant with high service and low prices, drawing customers away from both the bargain basement and carriage trade quadrants. The result for the stretched-out company is reduced profitability.

The company has two strategy decisions to make. One is to locate the center of gravity or core of the company's business along the axis. The other is to define the range along the axis it will cover.

The fundamental choice to be made is the selection of customers, for companies that reside in a given quadrant will *generally* produce orders in that quadrant. Customers in each quadrant of the profitability matrix behave in a distinctive manner. The supplier has to decide which behavior is most consistent with its strengths. For instance, in an industry with high transport costs, like cement or sand, a customer located at the maximum practical distance from your plant is likely to be in one of the right-hand quadrants—for you. For a competitor whose plant is located near the customer, that account will probably be in a left-hand quadrant. Unless you can form a carriage-trade relationship with that customer—realizing high prices because of the value of your services—you would do better to concede the account to your competitor.

Provide support systems. Unless it wants to follow a policy of cost-plus pricing, the company needs to develop processes and systems that will help it manage the profitability dispersion. The company's information system should produce reports based on order, customer, and segment profitability, not just

on sales. Management must be oriented toward lateral cooperation among functions. A procedure that simply rewards salespeople for high unit sales and manufacturing personnel for low-cost production is unlikely to lead to the most profitable order mix.

Price setting rates special attention. Companies that operate in the bargain basement and aggressive quadrants of the profitability matrix must often set up centralized offices to price large orders and screen customers' demands for services. A "special bids" group is often the only way to give the quick replies and careful analyses such orders require. Such a group can best balance financial implications, production and operating capacity, and customer needs, without giving away the store. Since carriage trade customers value the supplier's extra services, a cost-plus pricing policy may be appropriate for them. Finally, pricing for the trade in the passive quadrant has to be based on the value the customer places on the product.

The analysis, strategy, and customer negotiation functions must be kept separate. A men's and boys' coat manufacturer we know of is a good example of what happens when this rule is ignored. The owner's three sons headed divisions serving the department store, discount store, and export markets, while the owner himself managed the private-label business. He called on the three big general merchandise chains (Sears, Ward, and Penney), one of which gave him almost all of his business. The sons' divisions were very profitable, but the private-label unit was a big money loser.

Why was this so? Before a son went out to negotiate an order, the owner stressed the need to get high prices, keep costs reasonable, and secure orders that fit the company's abilities. The father analyzed large orders for profitability. But when the father went to talk to his biggest customer, no one pressured him to keep profits up. He consistently caved in to demands for lower prices, higher service, and better quality. His sons felt powerless to analyze his orders for profitability. The lesson: the same person should not set profit goals and negotiate with customers.

The more services a company provides, the more coordination is necessary among the engineers, field-service staff, and other functionaries in delivering the product and service. Likewise, the more a company increases its cost to serve, the more important interfunctional coordination becomes. Low-cost, low-price, low-service bargain basement operators don't need and can't afford elaborate logistics, field service, and other coordinating mechanisms. Carriage trade customers can't operate without them.

Deciding what strategic choices to make requires maintaining market research, pricing analysis, and cost-accounting functions. While these are high-leverage operations in which small investments can yield high returns, in hard times companies often view them as nonessential overhead expenses. This short-sighted attitude can be very damaging.

Repeat analysis regularly. A one-shot profit dispersion and strategy analysis is of little use. Buying behavior and migration patterns, like markets and competitors, are dynamic. Migration patterns gradually dilute a company's account selection and management policies.

For one equipment manufacturer, winning bids meant losing money.

Cumberland Metals (a disguised name) made pollution control components for the Big Three auto companies in the mid-1970s. Margins were very good, reflecting the high value the auto companies placed on the product, their lack of experience with pollution control, and the absence of competition. The entry of competitors in the early 1980s and, on the customers' part, a shift in influence from engineering to procurement staff signaled a fundamental migration in their buying behavior, but Cumberland management ignored the warning signs. This inattention caused long-standing customer relations problems and a prolonged earnings slump.

Cumberland Metals is unusual because it had only three large accounts. The loss of accounts and orders from the carriage trade quadrant is normally a matter of erosion.

How often a company should analyze profit dispersion and strategy depends on the rate of change in the market and in technology. In many cases, a once-a-year analysis integrated with the annual marketing plan makes sense. In high technology or other rapidly changing industries, a more frequent review may be better. In any case, the main difficulty lies in setting up good systems to track costs, prices, and prof-

its; once the supporting information is available, the analysis is not difficult to perform.

Manage the dispersion

A custom fabricator of industrial equipment, though operating at capacity, was losing money. The obvious problem was low price levels for the industry. Investigation, however, pointed to a mixture of poor pricing, poor cost estimating, and a lack of knowledge of profitability dispersion. Some bids were too aggressively priced: after winning contracts, the company then lost money on them. Executives had structured other bids to "make good money," basing them on inflated cost estimates. Astute competitors costed these bids better, handled the price negotiations more skillfully, and won the contracts. So the fabricator was winning only unprofitable bids.

The electrical products division of a large corporation, on the other hand, understood the importance of profitability analysis. It carefully analyzed its costs, developed a proactive pricing approach, and meticulously selected orders, products, and customers that fit its production competence and capacity. After a thorough before-and-after review, the financial analysis department at headquarters declared that the division had gone from a 5% loss to a 10% profit on sales in a glutted, static commodity market.

When meticulous analysis, a sensible strategy, and effective implementation are combined, a company can manage its profitability dispersion to generate profits, not just sales. ☟

Reprint 87513

Authors' note: For their help in developing this article, we thank Harvard Business School professors Thomas V. Bonoma, Robert J. Dolan, Robert S. Kaplan, and Arthur Schleifer, Jr., and Ronald M. Whitfield of Data Resources and McGraw-Hill.

Porsche on nichemanship

"If I were going to be a car, I'd be a Porsche."

Peter Schutz and Jack Cook

Interviewed by David E. Gumpert

HBR:
Porsche might be described as the epitome of a niche marketer, appealing to a narrow segment of financially successful individuals. How would you describe your customers and their perceptions of Porsche?

Peter Schutz:
Our customers' perception of us is something that we've given a great deal of thought to, and, interestingly enough, our customers seem to have a common denominator, almost independent of where they live in the world. They are people who have set for themselves what they perceive to be extraordinarily high personal and professional goals; they also see themselves pursuing these goals virtually without compromise. They may seem to be risk takers, but on closer examination they turn out not to be because these folks have done their homework. It seems like they are doing the unusual but that's only because somebody else hasn't really thought of it. Now, all of those elements are important, you see, because if our company is to be successful appealing to those kinds of folks, we have to come up to their expectations.

Our customers are people who place high expectations on themselves. And they expect no less from the companies and people with whom they associate. They may not care much about the bread or the bakery, but they have high expectations for their hobbies, or the clothes they wear, or the restaurants they go to, or the cars they drive. As a result, in positioning our company we have to strive to be what

HBR Associate Editor David E. Gumpert conducted these interviews with two Porsche top executives, Peter Schutz, chief executive of Porsche AG, and Jack Cook, president of Porsche Cars North America. Sally Seymour, associate in communication teaching at the Harvard Business School, assisted in editing the transcript.

these people are as individuals. That means, among car companies, we have very high goals. And we have to pursue those goals virtually without compromise.

I think your observation about risk taking applies to entrepreneurs; that is, they appear to be taking great risks, but because they know their territory well, the risk is reduced.

It's very easy to say that our customers tend to be professional athletes, entertainers, small businesspeople, or stockbrokers. But even when people who are our customers or are our potential customers work in large organizations – a big corporation or the U.S. Army or something – they nonetheless see themselves as entrepreneurs, as having a mission within that company, which they approach in a very entrepreneurial way. And they don't so much see themselves as a homogeneous part of a large organization but rather as an exception. That's the common denominator.

I've formulated the slogan that if you really want to understand our customers, you have to understand the phrase "if I were going to be a car, I'd be a Porsche." And that's the reason why our cars have no chrome, and no Star Wars instrument panel, and all that, because that's just not the kind of people our customers are. Our customers respect competence and thoroughness as opposed to flashiness and show. As a matter of fact, they abhor phony air scoops just as they abhor any phoniness in themselves.

What else about the product appeals to your special class of customers?

It's probably more like a piece of clothing or furniture than a method of transportation because it is something the owner actually wears and is seen in. Many of our cars are owned by people who really don't need a car to go anywhere. In other words, it's a little bit like a sailboat; you know, nobody uses a sailboat to go anywhere. They enjoy sailing. A lot of people own a Porsche because they enjoy driving. Just to get there, they could do it a lot less expensively. The car is an expression of themselves.

On paper, the cars all accelerate quickly and drive quite fast, but there is a great deal of difference between driving, say, the rear-engine, air-cooled 911 and the front-engine, water-cooled 928. You might drive both cars over the same roads and find that if you drive them full out they will get there in about the same time. But the difference is as marked to somebody who understands cars as the difference that exists between playing the same tune on a piano or on a clarinet—it's the same notes, it's the same melody, but it's totally different.

Porsche has been known as a product-oriented company, and you are talking about the product. But you are talking about the customer as well. Is it fair to say that the company was a product-oriented company and you've been trying to turn it into a marketing-oriented company?

No, I wouldn't say that. Today I asked Professor Porsche, who built the first car, how he ever came up with a Porsche 356, which was the original Porsche. He said: "We did no market research, we had no sales forecasts, no return-on-investment calculations. None of that. I very simply built my dream car and figured that there would be other people who share that dream." I don't really think that's any different from what I have just described to you when I talked to you about achievers—the kind of people who constitute our customers. What we are trying to do is match their dream.

Professor Porsche did have a market in mind. His market was people who shared his dream. [See the insert for a brief history of the company.]

Has that philosophy endured?

I really feel that over the years the management of this company, in all disciplines, has maintained a close enough contact with our customers that we truly know how they think; we haven't made too many mistakes. I spend about 25% of my time with customers—not only dealers but customers, people who come here to pick up their Porsches. In Germany, for example, 60% of all the Porsches that are bought are picked up at the factory by their owners. And I have many opportunities to lunch with them, or they come here to say hello, particularly the Americans. So I have a chance to listen to them. I hear some of the most interesting things.

One of the things I found out very quickly is that an amazing number of our customers are not automobile enthusiasts. A lot of them are, but an amazing number aren't. So I decided I'd better understand that. You know, why would people buy Porsches if they were not interested in automobiles, racing, or even learning how to drive? One day I met a lady who drove a 928, which is a rather expensive Porsche. She was a very successful career woman, and like many such folks who are our customers, she had a lot of everything in the world except time. And she also had a 14-year-old daughter whom she adored. She said, "Mr. Schutz, when I drive this car to the high school to pick my daughter up after school, I end up with five youngsters in the car. If I drive any other car, I can't even find her; she doesn't want to come home."

Professor Porsche had the benefit of a lot of previous experience in designing cars. He had been able to gauge consumer tastes—between his father's experience and his own.

He wasn't really thinking about gauging consumer tastes. When he actualized his dream, it automatically appealed to others like him. That was the basic concept. I don't know that he ever thought it through in exactly those terms, but he is a man with a great feel for things. And I don't know if he ever sat down and said, "I am now going to postulate that there are other people like me who have similar tastes." But in effect that's what he did.

One thing he emphasized from a marketing perspective early on is the importance of racing. How does racing fit into the niche-marketing effort?

We promote racing for three reasons. First, it is probably the single most effective way to do our advertising and public relations. It gets us free space in the auto enthusiasts' magazines.

The second factor is the contribution that it makes to our technical development. Solving problems on a race car occurs on a very accelerated schedule; it's almost like developing military hardware during wartime. As a result, we may have the opportunity to build a car to get more power out of it. For example, electronic fuel injection, electronic ignition, carbon fiber brakes were all things that were developed in the heat of competition and in a time frame that you couldn't do any other way. So it makes a very substantial contribution to our technical expertise.

Probably the most important dimension, though, from my point of view, is the contribution that racing makes to our corporate culture. The racing activity is highly visible, and it has a couple of characteristics that I find extremely valuable in achieving the kind of quality we want. One of them is the concept that work has to be ready on time. You have to develop a critical path and plan all of your material flow. Whether you do this formally or informally, you have to get your arms around the vital dimensions of the project. And, of course, it introduces the idea that you work until the job is done, not until it's quitting time. Our racing team would never think of going home just because it's evening. If there's a race the next day, the car has to be finished. And that gets transferred to other areas of the company. It becomes part of the fiber of the entire company.

What is it about racing that appeals to your achievement-oriented customers?

Racing is a good example of how we may appear to be taking risks. But if you do your homework and you've researched it thoroughly, then the risk of losing is not as great as it may seem. You're certainly not rolling the dice. Now, our customers do not expect us always to win, because no one wins all the time. But something our customers would not understand and that would damage our image is if we went out and competed without having done our homework. They would say, "Gee, I don't run my business that way, and I don't want to be associated with people like that." So racing is an opportunity for us to demonstrate our competence, to demonstrate the state of technology with which we're building their automobile.

Racing is important also for the reason that their children wouldn't be anxious to get in that car if it weren't for the racing. The link is definitely there.

And when the daughter says, "My mom has a Porsche," or "We're going to be picked up in the Porsche," that registers "racing" with the kids.

Exactly.

How has the company image changed over the years? Or has it?

I think the company and its customers have been remarkably constant, particularly given the turbulence in this industry in general. I mean, just look at the product—the 911, in its external form, has not changed substantially in 21 years. You know, that's not as unusual as some people would make it sound. The Chevrolet Camaro was in continuous production from 1967 until 1982.

And people don't notice that. The Corvette was in production from 1953 until it was changed recently. So the kind of car that appeals to this basic market tends to be relatively timeless when you have a successful model. It's not like general transportation.

You can think of the automobile industry as consisting of two components. On the one hand, there are what I would loosely classify as utility vehicles. These are vehicles that are built to be used: to go to work, to deliver the kids, to go shopping. Their manufacture is largely determined by facts in the environment: cost of fuel, required emission levels, average size of the family, average length of commute—and as those things change, they change. And that's where the big revolution has been, from the large cars to little cars.

The other class of vehicles, for lack of a better name, I would call nonutility vehicles—and these are your Porsches, BMWs, Mercedes, and for some, maybe, Cadillacs. These cars are built to be enjoyed instead of just used. Now, some of them are good only to enjoy because their utility is very limited. The appeal of these nonutility vehicles is not determined by facts, rather by feelings. And human feelings change on a totally different cadence from the facts and the environment.

For instance, there is no surer way to sell a Porsche than to make it burn less fuel and be more efficient. When someone says to a Porsche owner, "It must be great to drive a fast car like that, but I couldn't afford to buy the fuel," the owner can come back with "Hey, wait a minute. My car burns less fuel than your Volkswagen." And he explains how it's because of the electronic ignition and all that. "You see, I have a 928—big car, goes from 0 to 60 in six seconds, $22\frac{1}{2}$ miles per gallon, combined city and highway." See, that's incredible. That's important. Not because fuel costs money; that's got nothing to do with anything. But you see, that car is doing the kind of thing that its owners like to see in themselves, in their businesses, and in their lives.

Yes. Then the question is how do you get all that—those feelings and the concept—to the customer? We talked about racing and the focus on the product. But how do you get the word out to the kind of people who may not be all that much interested in racing?

We took a look at all the advertising that was being done with automobiles, and it all had a sameness to it. They were all pushing for performance, for the appearance, good handling, blah, blah, blah. So we thought, what can we do now? Do we say we've got more of all of that? No. We came up with an ad to tell people just about our company – the engineers and the cars they have designed. And that ad was aimed at people who didn't already know Porsche. It made people think, "This isn't just a car for people who like to drive fast. As a matter of fact, some of the things here that they are saying about how they run their business, that's how I try to run mine."

You indicated that Porsche is trying to increase its production.

Modestly. Because if we build too many cars, we will lose our exclusivity and cease being what we are. And we've got to be very conscious of that. We can only increase production if we add more models. We can't build more of what we already have. Because you get to see too many of them around, and all of a sudden it's nothing special.

Then how do you balance the desire for growth with the need to maintain an image of exclusivity?

That's very, very easy. You see, we have an unusual group of shareholders. All of the voting shares are in the hands of the Porsche family. And their priorities are very clear. Growth is simply not a prime objective of this business.

It is far more important to our shareholders to build the image and reputation of this company than it is to build the sales and profits. When the Porsche family hired me, they set no goal for growth or any objectives like that.

They want this company to be independent and to continue to be what it is and become more of what it is. But there's a limit to how much more

and at what rate we can become more of what we are, unless we decide to become something else.

One of the things, for example, that we're undertaking now is the development of an airplane engine. How in the world does an airplane engine fit into this business? Well, it fits a heck of a lot better than, for example, an economy sedan would. If we were a product-oriented company, we could say, "We know how to build cars, we know how to build an economy sedan, so let's do it." But you see, an economy sedan doesn't appeal to the customer group we have. The airplane engine does because a lot of the folks who drive our cars are also pilots, and they fly little airplanes. So now we've taken the engine out of their favorite car, and we're making an airplane engine out of it to sell to builders of private aircraft.

So when these airplane manufacturers sell their airplane they can say, "with a Porsche engine."

Exactly.

You seem to eschew growth in terms of maximizing profits and sales. What have been the financial results during the last three or four years?

Oh, I would say they've been satisfactory. The year that I joined the company it had a plan to earn 8 million deutsche marks after tax on sales of around 900 million deutsche marks. The most the company ever earned in one year after tax was something around 20 or 21 million.

Last year, ending July 31, 1985, we had sales of more than 3 billion marks. And we earned more than 92 million after tax. A 3 1/2% earnings as a percentage of sales is pretty respectable for a German company. This year, we will probably do 3 1/2 billion and do about 3.4% profit after tax. The company has no debt, and we finance everything out of continuing operations. We've invested three quarters of a billion deutsche marks in the last three years, and we are now in the middle of a three-year period where we invest a billion deutsche marks.

Then the company puts what could be higher profits into research, development, and improving facilities.

That's right.

How does Porsche stay competitive technically as such a small fish in a big pond?

Through outside engineering, which is the company's heritage. Today it really serves several, very specific purposes. One of them, of course, is that it makes money. It gives us a little more balance, something to lean on in the cyclicality of the automobile business.

The second thing is that we're a small company and yet do extremely progressive engineering. That requires the committed support of a lot of suppliers. And it is questionable whether – without outside engineering – we would get the support we need on the basis of the small quantities that we subsequently purchase from them. With the outside engineering – we do work for a lot of big companies, like Ford, General Motors, Volkswagen, Volvo, and many others – we get the committed support of suppliers who want to be part of that development in order to have the inside track for subsequent opportunities. When we get a request from Ford to take an engine and convert it from carburetor to fuel injection, Bosch works on that project with us so that it can later develop fuel injection equipment for millions of cars. Bosch is the biggest supplier of ignitions, motors, and batteries, and it's just three kilometers from here.

We have relationships with suppliers that far transcend our quantities. Outside engineering is the only way we get folks like that to help us develop pistons and other components for race cars.

Now, the third thing is that we have the best and most innovative engineers because the heart of this business is its technology. We attract and hold them with a very broad range of technical projects to work on, like styling the interior of the Airbus cockpit or designing, building, and supporting a Formula 1 racing engine.

We do a lot of work for other companies on improving performance of engines, or brakes, or transmissions – we design whole automobiles. We had a long project with Russia to design a small economy car like a Volkswagen Rabbit, which is a long way from a sports car.

So on the one hand, our engineers have a large variety of technical experience. On the other hand, they get to work with the Russians; they get to work with General Motors, with Ford, with Volkswagen, Mercedes, BMW – they have an opportunity to see how work is done in other countries, in other cultures, in other companies.

Now, both of those things provide a wonderfully varied environment, which plays an important role in making the job interesting, and you end up with an establishment that is multilingual and very experienced. They see how the organization is structured at other companies and how it's done in Russia. And then they're always thankful that they get to work here.

From auto design to mystique

When Ferdinand Porsche left Daimler-Benz in 1929 to start his own automobile design company in Stuttgart, he quickly widened his reputation as a creator of luxury and racing cars. He added a mass-market car to his credits as well – the auto that would eventually come to be known as the Volkswagen. During World War II, he designed military vehicles for the German army and became a confidant of Adolf Hitler.

Despite his growing renown, none of Porsche's designs carried his name until 1948, when his son, Ferry, started Porsche AG in Stuttgart to manufacture the first family-designed sports cars. The Porsche name carried weight in the marketplace as the new manufacturer carved out a niche as a producer of classically designed, high-performance sports cars. During the 1950s, it sold about 65% of its cars in the United States, and today the U.S. remains its largest market, absorbing more than half the 50,000 autos produced annually. The company has built on its reputation as a premier maker of sports cars in large measure because its racing cars regularly win European and American championships.

Though Ferry Porsche, now 76, still helps run the company, the chief executive's duties were assumed in 1981 by an American, Peter Schutz, who came to Porsche from Cummins Engine. Ironically, Schutz is not only an American, but a refugee of Nazi persecution – he fled Germany with his parents in 1939 because his father was Jewish.

Growth during the 1980s has been steady and substantial, from something less than 5,000 employees and 28,000 cars shipped in 1981 to 7,600 employees and 50,000 cars shipped in 1985. Of the company's annual $1 billion in revenues, about 80% come from autos and the remainder from engineering contracts and sale of spare parts.

As it was at the start in 1948, the high-priced, two-seat sports car is the mainstay of Porsche's business. It produces three basic models: the 944 at about $22,000, the 911 at $32,000, and the 928 at $50,000.

That brings me to the question of who comprises your competition.

Our competition really comes from two totally different places. For example, we compete with such things as sailboats, summer homes, and airplanes – discretionary purchases. But we have a big advantage with our customers in this area, because most of those objects require a lot of the one thing these folks don't have, and that's time. If you have a Porsche and make *it* your hobby, then you can enjoy it every day on your way to work and on your way to the airport, something you can't do with a sailboat or a summer home.

Then we compete with other automobile manufacturers. Here our three product lines compete very differently. The four-cylinder 944 has the most competition. It competes with everything from Corvettes, to Japanese cars, to Pontiac Fieros. So that's a very tough, competitive business. The six-cylinder 911, on the other hand, is unique. It drives like no other car and sounds like no other car. And we intend to keep it that way. The eight-cylinder 928, in turn, competes with Jaguars, Ferraris, the big Mercedes coupes, and now the new Cadillac, because it's a two-seater. So that's really a bit different segment.

Who are you most concerned about? I would guess that the Japanese look awfully threatening.

As long as we watch the quality of what we build, we have a leg up on building a good car.

You mean, from a technical standpoint?

The thing the Japanese do best, which is to build a large number of cars that are basically alike with flawless quality and for a good price, is not what appeals to our customers.

But how do you differentiate yourself from the Japanese—from the Mazda RX-7 and the Nissan 300ZX—in your potential customers' minds?

Well, I think our cars can do things theirs can't do. And the way you realize that is you drive them; they just don't feel the same. The difference is in the driving, not in how fast you get there and all those things.

It's not something you can describe quantitatively because it has to do with so many subtle things, and these are the things that we feel we can do best. So when you drive a Porsche, it's not like driving any other car; you can tell right away that you're in a Porsche.

Then how does marketing a premium-quality product differ from marketing a more ordinary, mass-produced type of product?

I really don't know how you market a mass product. I've never done it, so I don't pretend to be an expert in that. Actually, I find that marketing a Porsche is not all that different from when I was working for Cummins Engine and marketing truck engines. Truck drivers use the engines in their trucks in much the same way as Porsche owners use their Porsches. It's a very personal relationship, and it has to do with the way it sounds, the way it vibrates, the way it feels.

I would assume that the customers of a premium product are less price sensitive.

I think that's a misconception. You see, I know people who have owned a Porsche for ten years and sold it for the same amount that they bought it for. Because depreciation is so important in a car, they actually paid less than they would have if they had bought some economy car.

When I was still living in the United States, I bought a 1976 Corvette, and my friends said I was crazy. I spent $8,500 for a car. In 1976, that was a lot of dough. And they were buying little cars for $3,000 or $4,000. When I came to Germany in 1978, three years later, I sold the car for the same thing I paid for it. Their cars were junk! Three years later, they got a thousand or so on a trade-in. So I said, now, who has paid more money?

You think buyers of premium-quality products are aware of their investment?

Our buyers are very thoughtful people; they do not throw their money around. And if our cars were really that expensive, they wouldn't be buying them. It all depends on the used market, what we are doing to protect the price of a used Porsche, how we are supporting the product for the long term. Porsches, as you may not know, are made out of zinc-plated steel; they don't rust. We've had a seven-year rust guarantee on them; we're now going to ten years because we've never paid a claim. It works. And of course, more and more manufacturers are beginning to pick this up. But if you drive a Porsche for five years and you take decent care of it, it's going to be just as good as new.

It's a question of price to value. If that relationship is right, you'll get a high price for it.

How do you segment your specialized market?

We have a relatively homogeneous market. Fifty thousand cars—my God, that's one week's production for Chevrolet. In that sense, it's a relatively simple business. We wouldn't know where to start segmenting. Now, a lot of people drive a 944 because that's the least expensive Porsche, and it's the only one they can really afford. But once you get into the 911 and the 928 range, you're dealing with folks who can buy any car they want. They don't drive a 911 because they can't afford a 928. And they don't settle for a coupe instead of a convertible because the convertible costs 10% more.

How does Porsche's marketing, particularly with respect to distribution and advertising, differ

within the countries where they are sold? Germany vs. the United States, vs. France, for example? Or is there a commonality to all these things?

There's a commonality, and there's a lot of cultural difference. In other words, in America you do a lot more television. Of course, here in Germany, there is no advertising on television; there's no advertising on radio. In Germany, it's mostly newspapers and magazines. A lot of our advertising is really PR rather than ads. You know, reports about racing. And Porsche always seems to be an interesting subject. It's written about in magazines—*Road and Track, Motor Trend, Car and Driver*. They do feature stories, and they have told me that if Porsche is on the cover, the magazine automatically sells more copies. And almost every automotive publication has Porsche as a feature in its record-breaking edition.

But fundamentally, we now have control at the wholesale level in all our major markets: Germany, England, France, and America. Those four make up 85% of our business.

What do you mean you have control of the wholesale portion?

In the United States, until a year ago September, for example, Volkswagen of America was our importer, which in the growth phase of our company was probably a very good way of doing it. I think it helped both companies. As we've grown, though, we've just felt we had to have more say, particularly in the environment that we see ahead, which we think will require a lot more intensive customer contact than a mass producer can afford to do.

Now, you asked me, what do we have to do differently? Such things, for example, as order processing. The large variety of special items that our customers want to order—special paints, special seats—that are not in the catalog. We want people to be able to order almost anything, and we've structured the plant to be responsive to that—within a range that is technically sound.

You mean customizing?

That's correct. More custom tailoring. Particularly in the United States, Porsches have tended to be sold like other automobiles. That is, the importer would order so many of this color, so many of that color; then that's what was available for sale. Now we're creating a customer-driven order system.

Also, our customers would like to know when a car is going on the assembly line and when it's coming out. In the future, we might send the customer a letter that says, "Today your car was put into the plant. We expect it to be out next Tuesday." Then the customer might get another letter when it's on the ship about when it's expected to arrive. People want to know all those things. In the normal automotive distribution system, dealers have no way of determining this. So we think a lot of special services would enhance our ability to communicate with our customers and serve them.

I get the feeling that the U.S. subsidiary has a tremendous amount of autonomy in terms of marketing.

In each of our marketing territories, the responsibility lies with local managers. We act as a kind of U.S. board of directors, setting the policies. But the execution is largely in their hands. There are limits to what they can and cannot do because the image and reputation of this company are very important. A lot of practices that are acceptable in other branches of the automobile industry we would not find acceptable.

Like what?

Well, for example, if somebody started shouting from the rooftops that we've got 500 Porsches sitting here and they've all got to go by the end of next month. We don't want Porsches sold that way. We would like to build one less Porsche than the demand. If a dealer has cars it can't move, we'll take them and find a dealer that can move them.

Just one last question: Why not diversify into a four-seater or a sedan?

Well, I think right now we've got all we can handle. And the main reason that I have never looked at a four-seater is because I've never seen a four-seater that looks like a Porsche. It always ends up looking like some kind of sedan. We continue to do styling studies on how we can put more room in the backseat. But it can't end up looking like some kind of stretched-out coupe—you already see a lot of these. Because styling is very, very important.

Would a different style possibly dilute the Porsche image?

Very, very much so. I mean, if it doesn't fit into the scheme, it could be disastrous. I would say the 928, as a departure from the 911, gave this company a bad case of indigestion in the late 1970s. When I joined the company, we had a tough job learning how to position and sell that product. And we're still learning, because 928 customers are not 911 customers.

HBR:
Until December 1983, Volkswagen handled Porsche's distribution in the United States. Why did Porsche end the relationship?

Jack Cook:
We could see that General Motors was talking to Jaguar, that Honda and the British were getting together to build a car, that the Japanese were proceeding. Porsche wanted to make its distribution-marketing setup in the United States as good as the rest of its organization, so that four or five years from now when the competition gets better and better, we'll still be five years ahead of them, not only with our product and engineering but with our distribution.

What we want to do is not so much build more volume, because that could be counterproductive, but build stability into our organization and sales. Sales for Porsche have fluctuated during the last ten years; our objective here is to build gradually until we're selling about 30,000 to 35,000 cars a year in the United States. We saw that we needed to control our own destiny. The U.S. is our largest market. We have since implemented many changes to make life better for the customer.

What have you done?

Something, for example, that may seem routine and dull – how do you get a part for a vehicle needing service to the dealer so the customer doesn't have to wait very long? Most manufacturers, including our previous importer, give the dealer a monthly bulk order with the freight prepaid. Well, you might say, so what? That doesn't affect the customer. But it does, because some dealers tend to hold off on ordering until that bulk order comes due instead of paying the freight on a lot of orders throughout the month. Not that every dealer does that.

But to avoid that problem, we immediately put in a system of a weekly bulk order, which we

prepaid to the dealer, and would add a fifth one any time during the month, which we would prepay directly to the dealer. And if we make a mistake and don't have the part in our warehouses in the U.S., which are devoted exclusively to Porsche, then we say we made a mistake, and we ship that part via airfreight directly to the dealer from Stuttgart, West Germany. It takes four days to do it. So the result is not just better parts sales – that's not what we're interested in. The result is greater customer satisfaction.

What else have you done to improve your American operations?

We've invested in two, 100,000-square-foot parts warehouses – in Reno and in Charleston, South Carolina. We've also invested substantial amounts to make sure that the car is right when it arrives. Instead of using outside services to clean up the cars and send them to the dealers from the ports, we've established two predelivery inspection centers, also in Reno and Charleston. Their function is to check the cars from A to Z and make sure they are perfect so they can be shipped to the dealer and delivered to the customer. That's a little oversimplified, but not much. In effect, it's the end of the production line – the final inspection.

How did all that happen before you had these centers?

It was done in one of two ways. It was done in some parts of the country by outside services, and then in some parts – most of the country – by the dealers themselves. They got the car the way it came off the boat, covered with Cosmoline, maybe a scratch here, maybe an engine that needed tuning, etc.

Little irritations.

Yes. Now, maybe a dealer would do that job perfectly, if it was a quality dealer, and maybe it wouldn't. No one probably could do it quite as perfectly as we can, though, because by running all our cars through these two facilities we can afford to have the best equipment to do the checking and the repairs. Our dynamometer is the perfect way to check the engine output. Plus there's the human factor – people who do the same job and get good at it and see these cars all the time, instead of doing a variety of things, like working on a customer's car for two days, doing some predelivery on a car for half a day, and so forth. Our people specialize, and they get better, and they know what to look for.

What are you doing to involve dealers in your quality-improvement efforts?

We want to get some new thinking into the organization of 325 or so dealers. That's been one of my most difficult communications jobs. I have to tell them (in a warranty dispute), "Look, the fact that it is 75 miles over warranty doesn't really make a difference. It's something we did wrong that has broken. We want that customer looked after." Or if there's something wrong with the product or wrong with the way someone has been treated, we want to correct that. Automobile dealers of all makes have given this industry a bad name. And some of those dealers are selling Porsches today. We're doing our best to try to convince them that they should either stay with us and adopt this new philosophy – or sell a different product.

What is the extent of your investment in upgrading your American operation?

We've got two delivery centers (east and west), each worth about $7 million. That's just building and equipment with no staff. We've got total assets in the United States of more than $100 million.

What have you done to involve the dealers in your new parts and inspection facilities?

The dealers each have an IBM PC XT. We take the load on our Series 38 IBMs so that the dealer investment is low. And that means that dealers can call up on their PCs and determine where, for example, they can find a red car from a fellow dealer. If that dealer doesn't have a red car in stock, what do they do? They keep expanding the computer search to half the United States. They can also get right into our inventory and see what we have. So that's one area of helping customers, which I consider going beyond the guts and fundamentals and starting to get into frills.

The dealers can also process their warranties and order parts using the computer link. They can accomplish all these things in a very short period of time. I know one competitor that has been trying to get this system in for some 2$\frac{1}{2}$ years and has five dealers on it; we have every one of our dealers on the system.

What other marketing approaches are you considering in this country?

We intend to go on and do more things to enhance the purchase or the ownership of a Porsche. We've hired a special customer representative to go out and encourage and work with prime prospects: celebrities, executives at the top of *Fortune* "500" companies, top athletes, the kinds of people we see as our customers. We're going to help the dealers develop that business – not through price, but by telling these people

about the fun they could have with a Porsche and encouraging some of them to visit Germany and see our company, and so on.

And we've revamped our tourist delivery program. In the past, we've been a little constrained because of availability of product, but we're getting more production. Porsche AG has invested substantially in production capacity, which means we'll get 5,000 more cars this year. So we're using these extra cars to enhance the tourist delivery program – make more cars available to Americans in Stuttgart. The more high-profile Americans see how a Porsche is built, see the research-and-development facilities, and come home and talk to their friends about all of it at cocktail parties, the better it is for us. Word-of-mouth advertising is much more credible than advertising we pay for. Those are the kinds of things we intend to do. ▽

Father and son

Although I had the highest opinion in the world of my father's ability, and in fact regarded him as nothing short of a genius, our views on technical matters not infrequently clashed. I would hold opinions and ideas about some given subject that were completely the opposite of his, and I was just as convinced that I was right as he was that I was wrong! Of course, he always had on his side the unanswerable argument of far greater experience than mine; but if I expressed a view directly opposed to his when other people were present, then we would get into a fight. It was, I think, a matter of saving face on his part, but it didn't make things any easier....

I find it amusing to recall that if a discussion took place when the two of us were totally alone, my father not only would give me his complete attention, but would bear in mind what I had said, even though it might not have been his view in the first place. Then he would talk to our engineers and discuss with them what I had told him, but without revealing where the idea came from. For example, he would never say, "My son thinks this or that and believes we should try it out...." This situation often develops in a father-son relationship.

From
*We At Porsche:
The Autobiography of
Dr. Ing. h.c. Ferry Porsche
with John Bentley*
by John Bentley.
Copyright © 1976 by
Ferry Porsche and John Bentley.
Reprinted by permission of
Doubleday & Company, Inc.

Reprint 86211

David A. Garvin

Competing on the eight dimensions of quality

U.S. managers know that they have to improve the quality of their products because, alas, U.S. consumers have told them so. A survey in 1981 reported that nearly 50% of U.S. consumers believed that the quality of U.S. products had dropped during the previous five years; more recent surveys have found that a quarter of consumers are "not at all" confident that U.S. industry can be depended on to deliver reliable products. Many companies have tried to upgrade their quality, adopting programs that have been staples of the quality movement for a generation: cost of quality calculations, interfunctional teams, reliability engineering, or statistical quality control. Few companies, however, have learned to *compete* on quality. Why?

U.S. consumers doubt that U.S. companies can deliver quality.

Part of the problem, of course, is that until Japanese and European competition intensified, not many companies seriously tried to make quality programs work even as they implemented them. But even if companies *had* implemented the traditional principles of quality control more rigorously, it is doubtful that U.S. consumers would be satisfied today. In my

David A. Garvin is an associate professor of business administration at the Harvard Business School. He has published numerous articles on quality in HBR and other journals and is the recipient of McKinsey Awards for best HBR article in 1982 and 1983. This article draws from his book, Managing Quality, *to be published by Free Press.*

view, most of those principles were narrow in scope; they were designed as purely defensive measures to preempt failures or eliminate "defects." What managers need now is an aggressive strategy to gain and hold markets, with high quality as a competitive linchpin.

Quality control

To get a better grasp of the defensive character of traditional quality control, we should understand what the quality movement in the United States has achieved so far. How much expense on quality was tolerable? How much "quality" was enough? In 1951, Joseph Juran tackled these questions in the first edition of his *Quality Control Handbook*, a publication that became the quality movement's bible. Juran observed that quality could be understood in terms of avoidable and unavoidable costs: the former resulted from defects and product failures like scrapped materials or labor hours required for rework, repair, and complaint processing; the latter were associated with prevention, i.e., inspection, sampling, sorting, and other quality control initiatives. Juran regarded failure costs as "gold in the mine" because they could be reduced sharply by investing in quality improvement. He estimated that avoidable quality losses typically ranged from $500 to $1,000 per productive operator per year—big money back in the 1950s.

Reading Juran's book, executives inferred roughly how much to invest in quality improvement: expenditures on prevention were justified if they were lower than the costs of product failure. A corollary principle was that decisions made early in the production chain (e.g., when engineers first sketched out a product's design) have implications for the level of

"I spoke to my attorney today, Wendell, and I'm thinking of putting you into play."

quality costs incurred later, both in the factory and the field.

In 1956, Armand Feigenbaum took Juran's ideas a step further by proposing "total quality control" (TQC). Companies would never make high-quality products, he argued, if the manufacturing department were forced to pursue quality in isolation. TQC called for "interfunctional teams" from marketing, engineering, purchasing, and manufacturing. These teams would share responsibility for all phases of design and manufacturing and would disband only when they had placed a product in the hands of a satisfied customer--who remained satisfied.

Feigenbaum noted that all new products moved through three stages of activity: design control, incoming material control, and product or shopfloor control. This was a step in the right direction. But Feigenbaum did not really consider how quality was first of all a strategic question for any business; how, for instance, quality might govern the development of a design and the choice of features or options. Rather, design control meant for Feigenbaum mainly preproduction assessments of a new design's manufacturability, or that projected manufacturing techniques should be debugged through pilot runs. Materials control included vendor evaluations and incoming inspection procedures.

In TQC, quality was a kind of burden to be shared--no single department shouldered all the responsibility. Top management was ultimately accountable for the effectiveness of the system; Feigenbaum, like Juran, proposed careful reporting of the costs of

quality to senior executives in order to ensure their commitment. The two also stressed statistical approaches to quality, including process control charts that set limits to acceptable variations in key variables affecting a product's production. They endorsed sampling procedures that allowed managers to draw inferences about the quality of entire batches of products from the condition of items in a small, randomly selected sample.

Despite their attention to these techniques, Juran, Feigenbaum, and other experts like W. Edwards Deming were trying to get managers to see beyond purely statistical controls on quality. Meanwhile, another branch of the quality movement emerged, relying even more heavily on probability theory and statistics. This was "reliability engineering," which originated in the aerospace and electronics industries.

In 1950, only one-third of the U.S. Navy's electronic devices worked properly. A subsequent study by the Rand Corporation estimated that every vacuum tube the military used had to be backed by nine others in warehouses or on order. Reliability engineering addressed these problems by adapting the laws of probability to the challenge of predicting equipment stress.

Reliability engineering measures led to:

Techniques for reducing failure rates while products were still in the design stage.

Failure mode and effect analysis, which systematically reviewed how alternative designs could fail.

Individual component analysis, which computed the failure probability of key components and aimed to eliminate or strengthen the weakest links.

Derating, which required that parts be used below their specified stress levels.

Redundancy, which called for a parallel system to back up an important component or subsystem in case it failed.

Naturally, an effective reliability program required managers to monitor field failures closely to give company engineers the information needed to plan new designs. Effective field failure reporting also demanded the development of systems of data collection, including return of failed parts to the laboratory for testing and analysis.

Now, the proponents of all these approaches to quality control might well have denied that their views of quality were purely defensive. But what else was implied by the solutions they stressed – material controls, outgoing batch inspections, stress tests? Perhaps the best way to see the implications of their logic is in traditional quality control's most extreme form, a program called "Zero Defects." No other program defined quality so stringently as an absence of failures – and no wonder, since it emerged from the defense industries where the product was a missile whose flawless operation was, for obvious reasons, imperative.

In 1961, the Martin Company was building Pershing missiles for the U.S. Army. The design of the missile was sound, but Martin found that it could maintain high quality only through a massive program of inspection. It decided to offer workers incentives to lower the defect rate, and in December 1961, delivered a Pershing missile to Cape Canaveral with "zero discrepancies." Buoyed by this success, Martin's general manager in Orlando, Florida accepted a challenge, issued by the U.S. Army's missile command, to deliver the first field Pershing one month ahead of schedule. But he went even further. He promised that the missile would be perfect, with no hardware problems or document errors, and that all equipment would be fully operational 10 days after delivery (the norm was 90 days or more).

Quality means pleasing consumers, not just protecting them from annoyances.

Two months of feverish activity followed; Martin asked all employees to contribute to building the missile exactly right the first time since there would be virtually no time for the usual inspections. Management worked hard to maintain enthusiasm on the plant floor. In February 1962, Martin delivered on time a perfect missile that was fully operational in less than 24 hours.

This experience was eye-opening for both Martin and the rest of the aerospace industry. After careful review, management concluded that, in effect, its own changed attitude had assured the project's success. In the words of one close observer: "The one time management demanded perfection, it happened!"[1]

Martin management thereafter told employees that the only acceptable quality standard was "zero defects." It instilled this principle in the work force through training, special events, and by posting quality results. It set goals for workers and put great effort into giving each worker positive criticism. Formal techniques for problem solving, however, remained limited. For the most part, the program focused on motivation – on changing the attitudes of employees.

Strategic quality management

On the whole, U.S. corporations did not keep pace with quality control innovations the way a number of overseas competitors did. Particularly after World War II, U.S. corporations expanded rapidly and many became complacent. Managers knew that consumers wouldn't drive a VW Beetle, indestructible as it was, if they could afford a fancier car – even if this meant more visits to the repair shop.

But if U.S. car manufacturers *had* gotten their products to outlast Beetles, U.S. quality managers still would not have been prepared for Toyota Corollas – or Sony televisions. Indeed, there was nothing in the principles of quality control to disabuse them of the idea that quality was merely something that could hurt a company if ignored; that added quality was the designer's business – a matter, perhaps, of chrome and push buttons.

The beginnings of strategic quality management cannot be dated precisely because no single book or article marks its inception. But even more than in consumer electronics and cars, the volatile market in semiconductors provides a telling example of change. In March 1980, Richard W. Anderson, general manager of Hewlett-Packard's Data Systems Division, reported that after testing 300,000 16K RAM chips from three U.S. and three Japanese manufacturers, Hewlett-Packard had discovered wide disparities in quality. At incoming inspection, the Japanese chips had a failure rate of zero; the comparable rate for the three U.S. manufacturers was between 11 and 19 failures per 1,000. After 1,000 hours of use, the failure rate of the Japanese chips was between 1 and 2 per 1,000; usable U.S. chips failed up to 27 times per thousand.

Several U.S. semiconductor companies reacted to the news impulsively, complaining that the Japanese were sending only their best components to

1 James F. Halpin,
Zero Defects
(New York:
McGraw-Hill, 1966), p. 15.

the all-important U.S. market. Others disputed the basic data. The most perceptive market analysts, however, noted how differences in quality coincided with the rapid ascendancy of Japanese chip manufacturers. In a few years the Japanese had gone from a standing start to significant market shares in both the 16K and 64K chip markets. Their message – intentional or not – was that quality could be a potent strategic weapon.

U.S. semiconductor manufacturers got the message. In 16K chips the quality gap soon closed. And in industries as diverse as machine tools and radial tires, each of which had seen its position erode in the face of Japanese competition, there has been a new seriousness about quality too. But how to translate seriousness into action? Managers who are now determined to compete on quality have been thrown back on the old questions: How much quality is enough? What does it take to look at quality from the customer's vantage point? These are still hard questions today.

Some consumer preferences should be treated as absolute performance standards.

To achieve quality gains, I believe, managers need a new way of thinking, a conceptual bridge to the consumer's vantage point. Obviously, market studies acquire a new importance in this context, as does a careful review of competitors' products. One thing is certain: high quality means pleasing consumers, not just protecting them from annoyances. Product designers, in turn, should shift their attention from prices at the time of purchase to life cycle costs that include expenditures on service and maintenance – the customer's total costs. Even consumer complaints play a new role because they provide a valuable source of product information.

But managers have to take a more preliminary step – a crucial one, however obvious it may appear. They must first develop a clear vocabulary with which to discuss quality as *strategy*. They must break down the word quality into manageable parts. Only then can they define the quality niches in which to compete.

I propose eight critical dimensions or categories of quality that can serve as a framework for strategic analysis: performance, features, reliability, conformance, durability, serviceability, aesthetics, and perceived quality.[2] Some of these are always mutually reinforcing; some are not. A product or service can rank high on one dimension of quality and low on another – indeed, an improvement in one may be achieved

only at the expense of another. It is precisely this interplay that makes strategic quality management possible; the challenge to managers is to compete on selected dimensions.

---

1 Performance

Of course, performance refers to a product's primary operating characteristics. For an automobile, performance would include traits like acceleration, handling, cruising speed, and comfort; for a television set, performance means sound and picture clarity, color, and the ability to receive distant stations. In service businesses – say, fast food and airlines – performance often means prompt service.

Because this dimension of quality involves measurable attributes, brands can usually be ranked objectively on individual aspects of performance. Overall performance rankings, however, are more difficult to develop, especially when they involve benefits that not every consumer needs. A power shovel with a capacity of 100 cubic yards per hour will "outperform" one with a capacity of 10 cubic yards per hour. Suppose, however, that the two shovels possessed the identical capacity – 60 cubic yards per hour – but achieved it differently: one with a 1-cubic-yard bucket operating at 60 cycles per hour, the other with a 2-cubic-yard bucket operating at 30 cycles per hour. The capacities of the shovels would then be the same, but the shovel with the larger bucket could handle massive boulders while the shovel with the smaller bucket could perform precision work. The "superior performer" depends entirely on the task.

Some cosmetics wearers judge quality by a product's resistance to smudging; others, with more sensitive skin, assess it by how well it leaves skin irritation-free. A 100-watt light bulb provides greater candlepower than a 60-watt bulb, yet few customers would regard the difference as a measure of quality. The bulbs simply belong to different performance classes. So the question of whether performance differences are quality differences may depend on circumstantial preferences – but preferences based on functional requirements, not taste.

Some performance standards *are* based on subjective preferences, but the preferences are so universal that they have the force of an objective standard. The quietness of an automobile's ride is usually viewed as a direct reflection of its quality. Some people like a dimmer room, but who wants a noisy car?

---

2 This framework first appeared,
in a preliminary form,
in my article
"What Does 'Product Quality' Really Mean?"
Sloan Management Review, Fall 1984.

2 Features

Similar thinking can be applied to features, a second dimension of quality that is often a secondary aspect of performance. Features are the "bells and whistles" of products and services, those characteristics that supplement their basic functioning. Examples include free drinks on a plane, permanent-press cycles on a washing machine, and automatic tuners on a color television set. The line separating primary performance characteristics from secondary features is often difficult to draw. What is crucial, again, is that features involve objective and measurable attributes; objective individual needs, not prejudices, affect their translation into quality differences.

To many customers, of course, superior quality is less a reflection of the availability of particular features than of the total number of options available. Often, choice is quality: buyers may wish to customize or personalize their purchases. Fidelity Investments and other mutual fund operators have pursued this more "flexible" approach. By offering their clients a wide range of funds covering such diverse fields as health care, technology, and energy – and by then encouraging clients to shift savings among these – they have virtually tailored investment portfolios.

Employing the latest in flexible manufacturing technology, Allen-Bradley customizes starter motors for its buyers without having to price its products prohibitively. Fine furniture stores offer their customers countless variations in fabric and color. Such strategies impose heavy demands on operating managers; they are an aspect of quality likely to grow in importance with the perfection of flexible manufacturing technology.

3 Reliability

This dimension reflects the probability of a product malfunctioning or failing within a specified time period. Among the most common measures of reliability are the mean time to first failure, the mean time between failures, and the failure rate per unit time. Because these measures require a product to be in use for a specified period, they are more relevant to durable goods than to products and services that are consumed instantly.

Reliability normally becomes more important to consumers as downtime and maintenance become more expensive. Farmers, for example, are especially sensitive to downtime during the short harvest season. Reliable equipment can mean the difference between a good year and spoiled crops. But consumers in other markets are more attuned than ever to product reliability too. Computers and copying machines certainly compete on this basis. And recent market research shows that, especially for young women, reliability has become an automobile's most desired attribute. Nor is the government, our biggest single consumer, immune. After seeing its expenditures for major weapons repair jump from $7.4 billion in fiscal year 1980 to $14.9 billion in fiscal year 1985, the Department of Defense has begun cracking down on contractors whose weapons fail frequently in the field.

4 Conformance

A related dimension of quality is conformance, or the degree to which a product's design and operating characteristics meet established standards. This dimension owes the most to the traditional approaches to quality pioneered by experts like Juran.

All products and services involve specifications of some sort. When new designs or models are developed, dimensions are set for parts and purity standards for materials. These specifications are normally expressed as a target or "center"; deviance from the center is permitted within a specified range. Because this approach to conformance equates good quality with operating inside a tolerance band, there is little interest in whether specifications have been met exactly. For the most part, dispersion within specification limits is ignored.

One drawback of this approach is the problem of "tolerance stack-up": when two or more parts are to be fit together, the size of their tolerances often determines how well they will match. Should one part fall at a lower limit of its specification, and a matching part at its upper limit, a tight fit is unlikely. Even if the parts are rated acceptable initially, the link between them is likely to wear more quickly than one made from parts whose dimensions have been centered more exactly.

To address this problem, a more imaginative approach to conformance has emerged. It is closely associated with Japanese manufacturers and the work of Genichi Taguchi, a prizewinning Japanese statistician. Taguchi begins with the idea of "loss function," a measure of losses from the time a product is shipped. (These losses include warranty costs, nonrepeating customers, and other problems resulting from performance failure.) Taguchi then compares such losses to two alternative approaches to quality: on the one hand, simple conformance to specifications, and on the other, a measure of the degree to which parts or products diverge from the ideal target or center.

He demonstrates that "tolerance stack-up" will be worse – more costly – when the dimensions

| Exhibit | **Two approaches to conformance** |

In the following graphs, shaded areas under the curves indicate items whose measurements meet specifications. White areas indicate items not meeting specifications.

Production process 1

| Specification limit | Target | Specification limit |

1.35   1.40   1.45

In production process 1 (favored by Taguchi), items distribute closely around the target, although some items fall outside specifications.

Production process 2

| Specification limit | Target | Specification limit |

1.35   1.40   1.45

In production process 2 (favored in traditional approaches), items all distribute within specifications, but not tightly around the target.

Source: L.P. Sullivan, "Reducing Variability: A New Approach to Quality," *Quality Progress*, July 1984, p. 16.

ations from standard, like misspelled labels or shoddy construction, that do not lead to service or repair. In service businesses, measures of conformance normally focus on accuracy and timeliness and include counts of processing errors, unanticipated delays, and other frequent mistakes.

5   Durability

A measure of product life, durability has both economic and technical dimensions. Technically, durability can be defined as the amount of use one gets from a product before it deteriorates. After so many hours of use, the filament of a light bulb burns up and the bulb must be replaced. Repair is impossible. Economists call such products "one-hoss shays" (after the carriage in the Oliver Wendell Holmes poem that was designed by the deacon to last a hundred years, and whose parts broke down simultaneously at the end of the century).

In other cases, consumers must weigh the expected cost, in both dollars and personal inconvenience, of future repairs against the investment and operating expenses of a newer, more reliable model. Durability, then, may be defined as the amount of use one gets from a product before it breaks down and replacement is preferable to continued repair.

This approach to durability has two important implications. First, it suggests that durability and reliability are closely linked. A product that often fails is likely to be scrapped earlier than one that is more reliable; repair costs will be correspondingly higher and the purchase of a competitive brand will look that much more desirable. Because of this linkage, companies sometimes try to reassure customers by offering lifetime guarantees on their products, as 3M has done with its videocassettes. Second, this approach implies that durability figures should be interpreted with care. An increase in product life may not be the result of technical improvements or the use of longer-lived materials. Rather, the underlying economic environment simply may have changed.

For example, the expected life of an automobile rose during the last decade—it now averages 14 years—mainly because rising gasoline prices and a weak economy reduced the average number of miles driven per year. Still, durability varies widely among brands. In 1981, estimated product lives for major home appliances ranged from 9.9 years (Westinghouse) to 13.2 years (Frigidaire) for refrigerators, 5.8 years (Gibson) to 18 years (Maytag) for clothes washers, 6.6 years (Montgomery Ward) to 13.5 years (Maytag) for dryers, and 6 years (Sears) to 17 years (Kirby) for vacuum cleaners.[3] This wide dispersion suggests that durability is a potentially fertile area for further quality differentiation.

of parts are more distant from the center than when they cluster around it, even if some parts fall outside the tolerance band entirely. According to Taguchi's approach, production process 1 in the *Exhibit* is better even though some items fall beyond specification limits. Traditional approaches favor production process 2. The challenge for quality managers is obvious.

Incidentally, the two most common measures of failure in conformance—for Taguchi and everyone else—are defect rates in the factory and, once a product is in the hands of the customer, the incidence of service calls. But these measures neglect other devi-

6 Serviceability

A sixth dimension of quality is serviceability, or the speed, courtesy, competence, and ease of repair. Consumers are concerned not only about a product breaking down but also about the time before service is restored, the timeliness with which service appointments are kept, the nature of dealings with service personnel, and the frequency with which service calls or repairs fail to correct outstanding problems. In those cases where problems are not immediately resolved and complaints are filed, a company's complaint-handling procedures are also likely to affect customers' ultimate evaluation of product and service quality.

Some of these variables reflect differing personal standards of acceptable service. Others can be measured quite objectively. Responsiveness is typically measured by the mean time to repair, while technical competence is reflected in the incidence of multiple service calls required to correct a particular problem. Because most consumers equate rapid repair and reduced downtime with higher quality, these elements of serviceability are less subject to personal interpretation than are those involving evaluations of courtesy or standards of professional behavior.

Even reactions to downtime, however, can be quite complex. In certain environments, rapid response becomes critical only after certain thresholds have been reached. During harvest season, farmers generally accept downtime of one to six hours on harvesting equipment, such as combines, with little resistance. As downtime increases, they become anxious; beyond eight hours of downtime they become frantic and frequently go to great lengths to continue harvesting even if it means purchasing or leasing additional equipment. In markets like this, superior service can be a powerful selling tool. Caterpillar guarantees delivery of repair parts anywhere in the world within 48 hours; a competitor offers the free loan of farm equipment during critical periods should its customers' machines break down.

Customers may remain dissatisfied even after completion of repairs. How these complaints are handled is important to a company's reputation for quality and service. Eventually, profitability is likely to be affected as well. A 1976 consumer survey found that among households that initiated complaints to resolve problems, more than 40% were not satisfied with the results. Understandably, the degree of satisfaction with complaint resolution closely correlated with consumers' willingness to repurchase the offending brands.[4]

Companies differ widely in their approaches to complaint handling and in the importance they attach to this element of serviceability. Some do their best to resolve complaints; others use legal gimmicks, the silent treatment, and similar ploys to rebuff dissatisfied customers. Recently, General Electric, Pillsbury, Procter & Gamble, Polaroid, Whirlpool, Johnson & Johnson, and other companies have sought to preempt consumer dissatisfaction by installing toll-free telephone hot lines to their customer relations departments.

7 Aesthetics

The final two dimensions of quality are the most subjective. Aesthetics—how a product looks, feels, sounds, tastes, or smells—is clearly a matter of personal judgment and a reflection of individual preference. Nevertheless, there appear to be some patterns in consumers' rankings of products on the basis of taste. A recent study of quality in 33 food categories, for example, found that high quality was most often associated with "rich and full flavor, tastes natural, tastes fresh, good aroma, and looks appetizing."[5]

The aesthetics dimension differs from subjective criteria pertaining to "performance"—the quiet car engine, say—in that aesthetic choices are not nearly universal. Not all people prefer "rich and full" flavor or even agree on what it means. Companies therefore have to search for a niche. On this dimension of quality, it is impossible to please everyone.

8 Perceived quality

Consumers do not always have complete information about a product's or service's attributes; indirect measures may be their only basis for comparing brands. A product's durability, for example, can seldom be observed directly; it usually must be inferred from various tangible and intangible aspects of the product. In such circumstances, images, advertising, and brand names—inferences about quality rather than the reality itself—can be critical. For this reason, both Honda—which makes cars in Marysville, Ohio—and Sony—which builds color televisions in San Diego—have been reluctant to publicize that their products are "made in America."

Reputation is the primary stuff of perceived quality. Its power comes from an unstated anal-

3 Roger B. Yepsen, Jr., ed., *The Durability Factor* (Emmaus, Penn: Rodale Press, 1982), p. 190.

4 TARP, *Consumer Complaint Handling in America: Final Report* (Springfield, Va.: National Technical Information Service, U.S. Department of Commerce, 1979).

5 P. Greg Bonner and Richard Nelson, "Product Attributes and Perceived Quality: Foods," in *Perceived Quality*, ed. Jacob Jacoby and Jerry C. Olson (Lexington, Mass.: Lexington Books, D.C. Heath, 1985), p. 71.

ogy: that the quality of products today is similar to the quality of products yesterday, or the quality of goods in a new product line is similar to the quality of a company's established products. In the early 1980s, Maytag introduced a new line of dishwashers. Needless to say, salespeople immediately emphasized the product's reliability—not yet proven—because of the reputation of Maytag's clothes washers and dryers.

Competing on quality

This completes the list of the eight dimensions of quality. The most traditional notions—conformance and reliability—remain important, but they are subsumed within a broader strategic framework. A company's first challenge is to use this framework to explore the opportunities it has to distinguish its products from another company's wares.

The quality of an automobile tire may reflect its tread-wear rate, handling, traction in dangerous driving conditions, rolling resistance (i.e., impact on gas mileage), noise levels, resistance to punctures, or appearance. High-quality furniture may be distinguished by its uniform finish, an absence of surface flaws, reinforced frames, comfort, or superior design.

One company's quality niche may be another's trap.

Even the quality of a less tangible product like computer software can be evaluated in multiple dimensions. These dimensions include reliability, ease of maintenance, match with users' needs, integrity (the extent to which unauthorized access can be controlled), and portability (the ease with which a program can be transferred from one hardware or software environment to another).

A company need not pursue all eight dimensions simultaneously. In fact, that is seldom possible unless it intends to charge unreasonably high prices. Technological limitations may impose a further constraint. In some cases, a product or service can be improved in one dimension of quality only if it becomes worse in another. Cray Research, a manufacturer of supercomputers, has faced particularly difficult choices of this sort. According to the company's chairman, if a supercomputer doesn't fail every month or so, it probably wasn't built for maximum speed;

in pursuit of higher speed, Cray has deliberately sacrificed reliability.

There are other trade-offs. Consider the following:

☐   In entering U.S. markets, Japanese manufacturers often emphasize their products' reliability and conformance while downplaying options and features. The superior "fits and finishes" and low repair rates of Japanese cars are well known; less often recognized are their poor safety records and low resistance to corrosion.

☐   Tandem Computers has based its business on superior reliability. For computer users that find downtime intolerable, like telephone companies and utilities, Tandem has devised a fail-safe system: two processors working in parallel and linked by software that shifts responsibility between the two if an important component or subsystem fails. The result, in an industry already well-known for quality products, has been spectacular corporate growth. In 1984, after less than 10 years in business, Tandem's annual sales topped $500 million.

☐   Not long ago, New York's Chemical Bank upgraded its services for collecting payments for corporations. Managers had first conducted a user survey indicating that what customers wanted most was rapid response to queries about account status. After it installed a computerized system to answer customers' calls, Chemical, which banking consumers had ranked fourth in quality in the industry, jumped to first.

☐   In the piano business, Steinway & Sons has long been the quality leader. Its instruments are known for their even voicing (the evenness of character and timbre in each of the 88 notes on the keyboard), the sweetness of their registers, the duration of their tone, their long lives, and even their fine cabinet work. Each piano is built by hand and is distinctive in sound and style. Despite these advantages, Steinway recently has been challenged by Yamaha, a Japanese manufacturer that has built a strong reputation for quality in a relatively short time. Yamaha has done so by emphasizing reliability and conformance, two quality dimensions that are low on Steinway's list.

These examples confirm that companies can pursue a selective quality niche. In fact, they may have no other choice, especially if competitors have established reputations for a certain kind of excellence. Few products rank high on all eight dimensions of quality. Those that do—Cross pens, Rolex watches, Rolls-Royce automobiles—require consumers to pay the cost of skilled workmanship.

6 Consumer Network, Inc.,
Brand Quality Perceptions
(Philadelphia: Consumer Network, August 1983),
                                            p. 17 and 50-51.

Strategic errors

A final word, not about strategic opportunities, but about the worst strategic mistakes. The first is direct confrontation with an industry's leader. As with Yamaha vs. Steinway, it is far preferable to nullify the leader's advantage in a particular niche while avoiding the risk of retaliation. Moreover, a common error is to introduce dimensions of quality that are unimportant to consumers. When deregulation unlocked the market for residential telephones, a number of manufacturers, including AT&T, assumed that customers equated quality with a wide range of expensive features. They were soon proven wrong. Fancy telephones sold poorly while durable, reliable, and easy-to-operate sets gained large market shares.

Shoddy market research can add quality features nobody wants.

Shoddy market research often results in neglect of quality dimensions that *are* critical to consumers. Using outdated surveys, car companies overlooked how important reliability and conformance were becoming in the 1970s; ironically, these companies failed consumers on the very dimensions that were key targets of traditional approaches to quality control.

It is often a mistake to stick with old quality measures when the external environment has changed. A major telecommunications company had always evaluated its quality by measuring timeliness — the amount of time it took to provide a dial tone, to connect a call, or to be connected to an operator. On these measures it performed well. More sophisticated market surveys, conducted in anticipation of the industry's deregulation, found that consumers were not really concerned about call connection time; consumers assumed that this would be more or less acceptable. They were more concerned with the clarity of transmission and the degree of static on the line. On these measures, the company found it was well behind its competitors.

In an industry like semiconductor manufacturing equipment, Japanese machines generally require less set-up time; they break down less often and have few problems meeting their specified performance levels. These are precisely the traits desired by most buyers. Still, U.S. equipment can *do* more. As one U.S. plant manager put it: "Our equipment is more advanced, but Japanese equipment is more developed."

Quality measures may be inadequate in less obvious ways. Some measures are too limited; they fail to capture aspects of quality that are important for competitive success. Singapore International Airlines, a carrier with a reputation for excellent service, saw its market share decline in the early 1980s. The company dismissed quality problems as the cause of its difficulties because data on service complaints showed steady improvement during the period. Only later, after SIA solicited consumer responses, did managers see the weakness of their former measures. Relative declines in service had indeed been responsible for the loss of market share. Complaint counts had failed to register problems because the proportion of passengers who wrote complaint letters was small — they were primarily Europeans and U.S. citizens rather than Asians, the largest percentage of SIA passengers. SIA also had failed to capture data about its competitors' service improvements.

The pervasiveness of these errors is difficult to determine. Anecdotal evidence suggests that many U.S. companies lack hard data and are thus more vulnerable than they need be. One survey found that 65% of executives thought that consumers could readily name — without help — a good quality brand in a big-ticket category like major home appliances. But when the question was actually posed to consumers, only 16% could name a brand for small appliances, and only 23% for large appliances.[6] Are U.S. executives that ill-informed about consumers' perceptions? The answer is not likely to be reassuring.

Managers have to stop thinking about quality merely as a narrow effort to gain control of the production process, and start thinking more rigorously about consumers' needs and preferences. Quality is not simply a problem to be solved; it is a competitive opportunity. ∇

Reprint 87603

Reaching and
Cultivating Customers

Build customer relationships that last

Barbara Bund Jackson

How close can industrial marketers get to their customers— and for how long?

Marketing has long emphasized the importance of being close to the customer. But how close can a marketer realistically get to its customers? For what duration? And under what circumstances will customers make strong commitments to individual vendors? When, instead, will customers prefer weaker ties, perhaps to a number of different sellers? In reporting on a research project that explored long-term relationships between industrial customers and their suppliers, this author responds to the foregoing and other questions regarding patterns of customer-vendor behavior. Building and maintaining lasting customer ties, she suggests, involves doing a number of things right, consistently, over time. It takes coordination on the part of the seller of resources and tools to meet the customer's future as well as its immediate needs.

Ms. Jackson is vice president of Index Systems, a consulting firm headquartered in Cambridge, Massachusetts that specializes in the use of information and information technology for competitive advantage and for building customer relationships. She conducted the bulk of the research from which this article is drawn while on the faculty of the Harvard Business School. This article, her fourth for HBR, is based on her book, Winning and Keeping Industrial Customers: The Dynamics of Customer Relationships *(Lexington Books, 1985).*

Illustrations by Katherine Mahoney.

Scene 1: The executive committee meeting ends at 5:30 p.m. and the committee members adjourn, pleased with what they have accomplished. Their company, Superior Shipping Services, provides trucking to large industrial users, giving customers reliable scheduling and careful handling.

In response to decreased regulation in trucking and related industries, Superior's executives believe their company needs a stronger marketing orientation. They want to build and maintain lasting—and profitable—relationships with their customers. That, they believe, is what getting "close to the customer" means.

At an earlier meeting, the executive committee had decided to recruit a sales-marketing manager from a renowned marketer in the computer industry. Superior's president argued that such a person was likely to have attitudes and values that would fit well with the company's reputation for especially high quality and service.

The president and administrative vice president then identified possible candidates. The leading choice was Dale Spencer, a senior salesperson with an impressive record. At this meeting, the committee has outlined an offer that Superior's president believes would be attractive to Spencer.

Scene 2 (one month later): Dale Spencer assumes the job of vice president—sales for Superior Shipping. The negotiations have been smooth and Spencer is pleased. Spencer and Superior's president have agreed completely on what Spencer ought to do.

In the past, Spencer had been a patient and successful builder of customer relationships. On occasion, sales efforts became protracted as Spencer and other support people devoted long hours to wooing prospects. They eventually won most of the orders— and the resulting relationships proved close and highly satisfactory to both parties.

Superior's managers want similar customer ties. They plan to invest time and effort in studying their customers' shipping needs. They will help customers plan. They will also maintain the high quality of Superior's service. As a result, they expect to maintain—indeed, strengthen—Superior's relationships with its existing customers. They also expect to win important new customers.

Spencer will have responsibility for instilling the new attitude and approach in Superior's sales force. Spencer will also personally handle sales efforts at some of the key new accounts. Spencer is excited about the challenge.

Author's note: The Superior Shipping Services example is hypothetical but built around elements of several actual field situations. The individuals described are fictitious.

Scene 3 (two years later): Several of Superior Shipping's important executives are discussing Dale Spencer's future with the company. Spencer has been severely disappointed with the results to date. The executives, knowing that Spencer may leave, are thinking about whether to encourage or discourage the change. They wonder what has happened at Superior—and why.

Spencer has been a respected manager. The salespeople have indeed learned better ways of analyzing customers' long-term shipping requirements and of identifying opportunities for improving them. Superior's other managers have kept more in touch with customers as part of the overall sales effort; they have heard numerous compliments about their salespeople—and especially about Dale Spencer.

Yet all these efforts have not produced more sales. True, many prospects have responded to Superior's attention by awarding the company some business. But many of those new customers—as well as many of Superior's old accounts—have also experimented with other shippers.

One competitor, Efficiency Truckers, has proven especially irksome, competing on the basis of price and doing so increasingly effectively. Many of Superior's established customers have given Efficiency their largest and most regular shipments in exchange for price concessions. Three of the company's most desired new customers have done the same thing even after Superior salespeople had helped them create their shipment patterns through consolidation and more careful planning.

Virtually all those customers have also continued to do some business with Superior, giving the company their last-minute smaller shipments, severely testing Superior's ability to provide quality service. Superior's revenue has slipped, its sales force expenses have increased, and all of Superior's managers are deeply concerned by the developments. Dale Spencer is especially upset by them.

What happened?

Close relationships

Superior's managers did not adequately consider the differences between the market for computers and the market for shipping services, from the customers' point of view. They wanted to be close to the customer, but close to the customer means different things in the two marketplaces. The Superior example is especially instructive because a surprising number of marketers don't probe deeply enough into the nature of their relationships with customers. They want very much to believe that they're building lasting ties with buyers—but they're not. They want very much to do what I call "relationship marketing"—but their customers think more in terms of "transaction marketing."

Also, surprisingly, the distinctions between relationship marketing and transaction marketing are not clear, partly because successful relationship marketing is so complex and also because so many complicated and hard (or impossible) to measure factors determine what is appropriate to a situation, whether relationship marketing, transaction marketing, or something in between.

Because marketing practice and the marketing literature have devoted more attention to transaction marketing, this article and the research project on which it is based (see the insert) instead emphasize lasting relationship marketing between industrial companies and their customers. Accordingly, I first contrast customer behavior in the markets for computers and for shipping services, and then I consider a wider variety of customer behavior.

Customer commitments

A customer for medium-size or large computer systems generally commits strongly to the vendor that provides the important parts of the system and that thereby defines the technical parameters of the installation. When a company chooses such a lead vendor, it generally expects to continue with that supplier for an extended period. In short, it expects a relationship.

The costs and pain of changing computer suppliers have led to this pattern. Most users are well aware of the expense and tumult involved in transferring programs from one computer to another; many have first-hand experience with the trauma. Further, leading computer vendors facilitate software conversions from one to another of their own machines, thus making it much easier for customers to remain with current suppliers than to switch.

Because commitments from their customers usually last a long time, mainframe computer vendors have been able to take a long view of their customers' relationships. They have sensibly invested up-front resources to win commitments, helped customers with long-term planning for computers, and generally acted as if their customer relationships would continue. For them, relationship marketing has been a sound choice.

By contrast, customers for shipping services can easily share their business among multiple suppliers. A customer can award a small initial order to a new supplier. If all goes well, the customer can award more business to the supplier; if not, the damage from using the new supplier has been contained. In turn, a successful new vendor may find that yet another competitor will win away some of its business from the same customer.

The seller of shipping services cannot necessarily justify up-front investments to win accounts. The seller cannot assume that by helping customers plan for their longer run needs it will gain a principal role in executing the long-term plan. Customers may gratefully accept the planning help today but, if switching costs are low, they may accept concessions from another source tomorrow.

Transaction marketing is appropriate here; relationship marketing can be dangerous. Perhaps Dale Spencer failed because he never understood transaction marketing.

Spectrum of behavior

In many situations, sellers will benefit from an examination of the commitments they enjoy from customers, including consideration of the closeness of their ties with them and the time horizon their customers use in their commitments. Some sellers will identify strong ties that they expect to last – like those in the computer example. Others will find weaker, more transient affiliations – like those in shipping. Others may identify intermediate or even more extreme patterns.

The foregoing leads us into two simplified pictures or models of accounts' possible behavior that can be considered as the end points of a spectrum. Accounts in real situations will generally occupy less radical positions along the spectrum.

Always-a-share model

One extreme is what I call the "always-a-share model," which assumes that a customer making purchases of some product category repeatedly can easily switch part or all of its patronage from one vendor to another. The customer can therefore share its patronage among multiple suppliers. Though extreme, this model suggests the actual behavior of some buyers of commodity chemicals, some apartment building owners who purchase major appliances, some buyers of computer terminals, and some mailing services and shipping services customers.

Because the always-a-share customer faces low switching costs, a vendor can sensibly assume that it has a chance of winning business from

such an account – provided that the seller offers an immediate attractive combination of product, price, support, and/or other benefits. The seller is not locked into an account from which it currently enjoys patronage, nor is it locked out of one to which it does not now sell.

In some situations suggesting always-a-share behavior, a customer may make a series of purchases each from a single supplier but sharing its patronage among vendors over time (e.g., a purchaser of simple machine tools). In other situations suggesting the always-a-share model, the product is more divisible and the customer shares its business among multiple vendors at one time (e.g., a purchaser of carbon steel).

Implications of always-a-share
The always-a-share buyer is likely to have a short time horizon in its ties with suppliers. Even vendors who make consistent sales to that customer are obliged to give good immediate reasons for continuing the relationship with each purchase.

Transaction marketing is apt for the always-a-share customer.

Lost-for-good model

The opposite end of the behavior spectrum also assumes a series of purchases over time, but it presumes that at any one time the account is committed to only one vendor. The account faces high costs of switching vendors and therefore changes only reluctantly. As a result, it is likely to remain committed to its current supplier.

If the account does leave a vendor, it is at least as hard to win back as it was to win in the first place. I call such behavior the "lost-for-good model," emphasizing the pain of losing such a customer. The flip side is more cheerful; once won this type of customer is likely to be won for a long time.

The behavior picture in this lost-for-good model is indeed extreme. It is also a reasonable simplification for actual situations in which switching vendors involves considerable cost and disruption. The model suggests the behavior of some but not all purchasers of, for example, computers, communications equipment, office automation systems, heavy construction equipment, magazine fulfillment services, and aircraft engines.

Implications of lost-for-good
The essence of this model is that since the account cannot easily switch its patronage, it will therefore view its commitment to a vendor as permanent and use a long time horizon in the relationship. In choosing a supplier, it will consider the seller's likely

Research design

This article is based on a research project that explored long-term relationships between industrial customers and their vendors. In my fieldwork, which included companies dealing with a variety of products, I compared the findings with existing marketing research that focuses on individual sales and short-term relationships.

I carried out extensive (multihour) interviews with managers about their organizations' histories of purchases and usage of communications equipment (PBXs and related products) and of computers. The sample included 11 customers of communications equipment and 16 computer purchasers. In half the organizations, I held interviews with at least 2 managers; in 2 companies, I conducted 3 separate interviews. In interviews with 6 potential customers, I explored office automation and local area networks; 3 customer interviews concerned purchases of supplies for offset platemakers.

I talked with approximately 35 industry experts and vendors' representatives, covering each product area. (I did not include vendor representatives, however, if legal and regulatory concerns made them reluctant to talk about how their organizations built and maintained strong ties with customers.) In numerous briefer and less formal discussions, I explored the application of the ideas presented here in other product marketplaces.

future abilities to satisfy its needs and it will not focus exclusively on the seller's immediate capabilities and inducements.

Because the customer takes a long time horizon, an industrial marketer can also sensibly take a long-term view of the relationship. Often the seller can justify heavy up-front investment in trying to win new (or significantly increased) commitments from such customers.

Relationship marketing is apt for the buyer who might be lost-for-good.

Intermediate types

Real customers are likely to approximate various spectrum points between lost-for-good and always-a-share. The position of a certain customer will depend in part on characteristics of the product category, on the customer's usage system for the product, and on actions both the vendor and the customer take. Examples of such customers are fleet purchasers of cars or trucks, buyers of carbon steel, and users of banking services.

At first glance, a fleet purchaser is appropriately placed near the always-a-share end of the behavior spectrum: the buyer could use products from several vendors and could switch its patronage easily. Other factors, however, might move fleet buyers somewhat closer to the lost-for-good model. A customer's in-house maintenance staff might be skilled in working on a particular vendor's products; mixing vendors might require retraining. Similarly, if a vendor designed its products to use a common set of parts, the customer who uses one vendor could save on spare parts inventory (and/or could reduce the time required to obtain needed parts). Thus while some fleet purchasers would be close to the always-a-share model, vendor actions and buyer investments would move others to the middle of the behavior spectrum—or even beyond.

In a similar way, a purchaser of carbon steel might appear to be the prototypical always-a-share buyer, able to mix and match suppliers even within a single time period. Many purchasers would indeed approximate that model. Consider, however, a steel user that is adopting a just-in-time system for its materials and component inventories. Just-in-time requires extremely close cooperation and scheduling between buyer and seller; it will usually work much more smoothly with a single supplier per time period. Moreover, once a supplier and buyer have learned to work well together, the buyer will be reluctant to change and have to orient a new vendor. Hence even for a commodity such as carbon steel, the customer's usage pattern and the vendor's investment in adapting to the buyer's procedures can create behavior more like lost-for-good.

Finally, look at a customer for banking services. Again, it would appear that a company (or individual) could conduct business simultaneously with several banks—perhaps using checking accounts in multiple banks. While some banking customers do so, other corporate financial managers save time and money by using integrated financial packages from their banks. Along with the savings they gain, they establish closer ties to the bank—and end up in the middle of the behavior spectrum.

It is important to note that positions are determined in part by vendor actions. Marketers can consequently benefit from understanding their own customers' positions—for two reasons.

First, diagnosis with regard to the spectrum can help sellers understand their customers' concerns and interests. It can, for example, help them identify the issues that will determine purchase decisions. An always-a-share customer will almost certainly emphasize shorter term, more immediate concerns. A lost-for-good account will place considerable emphasis on longer term issues, like the seller's ability to provide an ongoing stream of suitable products and to facilitate graceful upgrades from one product to another as ap-

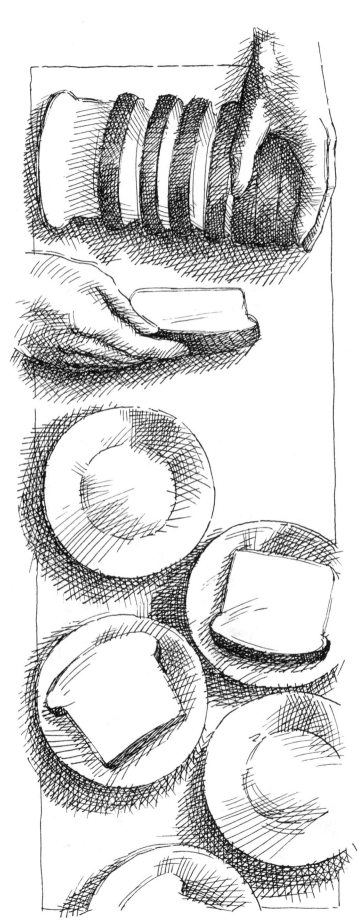

propriate over time. Such a customer will not ignore more immediate concerns, but it will not emphasize those considerations exclusively.

Second, the behavior spectrum can help vendors evaluate possible marketing strategies. Obviously, marketing actions that are well suited to customers toward one side of the spectrum will not necessarily be at all appropriate for customers toward the opposite end. In addition, the spectrum can help marketers evaluate the potential impact of marketing actions on moving customers closer to one end of the spectrum or the other.

Costs of change

An important point about switching costs is that customers face such costs in making many types of changes, regardless of whether a vendor change is involved. For example, a computer user faces some switching costs to modify existing programs even in changing from one operating system to another with the same vendor. In a similar way, a customer often faces switching costs when its vendor institutes new procedures – even if those procedures eventually improve service to the customer. For example, a supplier of manufactured parts may install an efficient new system for entering orders and for tracing previous orders. While the intended result is better service, the change will require an adjustment on the part of the customer.

In considering possible changes from one selling company to another, a customer will consider the relative switching costs (or savings) of the available choices. Therefore, marketers should consider both the absolute and the relative levels of disruption that changes will mean for the customer. The seller may find it useful to design its products and services so as to reduce switching costs that customers will face if they stay with that seller. To put it another way, the marketer should try to get the costs of intra-vendor switches considerably lower than the costs of inter-vendor changes.

Investment actions

The first, most obvious types of switching costs are the investments of time and money that customers must make to adapt to new products, services, or systems. Customers invest in their relationships with vendors in a variety of ways. They invest *money*; they invest in *people*, as in training employees to run new equipment; they invest in *lasting assets,* such as the equipment itself; and they invest in changing basic business *procedures* like inventory handling.

Naturally, the larger and more disruptive the investment actions required, the greater customer reluctance to change commitments and incur switching costs. Reluctance is especially high to abandoning previous investments in dollars, people, lasting assets, or procedures.

The amounts spent on products, being the only type of switching costs that can usually be determined precisely, are often emphasized in procurement evaluations. Other types of investments, however, can be more disruptive for the customer—and therefore can be more important switching costs. My field investigation suggests that past investments in procedures are particularly likely to create inertia against change.

For example, in adopting a comprehensive office automation system, many organizations must undergo thorough revisions in their procedures. The effects of change will reach widely throughout their organizations. As a result, many managers are wary of making mistakes; they want to move slowly into office automation. They especially want to avoid errors that would require yet another round of investments in procedures.

In the same way, because of past investments, buyers may be reluctant to incur the switching costs of modifying or replacing lasting assets. Computer software programs act as lasting assets. So do pieces of industrial equipment adapted to raw materials from a particular vendor.

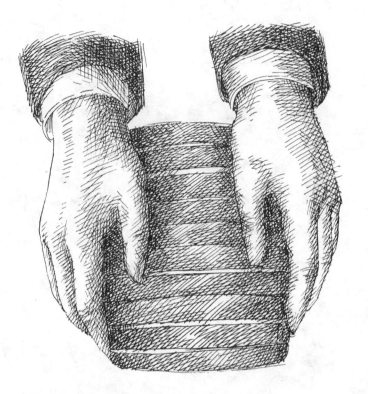

Risk or exposure

The second major category of switching costs concerns risk or exposure—that is, the danger to customers of making bad choices. While obviously not as immediately tangible or quantifiable as investments in time and money, the risks involved in switching can be just as important in determining customer behavior.

The immediate risks involved in changes frequently concern performance—that is, whether a purchase will work as intended and for the intended cost. Fear of immediate disruption and unsatisfactory performance can make a customer reluctant to change. Customers will feel more exposed when they buy products important to their own operations, when they buy from less well-known and less-established vendors, and when they buy complex and difficult-to-understand products. For the short run, a manager or an organization may feel considerably safer with the status quo—with not fixing something that is not demonstrably broken.

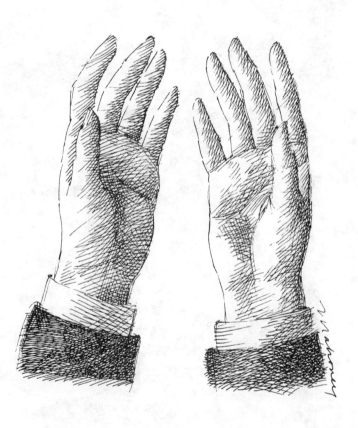

For the long run, however, customers often face risks in not changing. Fear of exposure can interfere with an organization's willingness and ability to adapt to external changes and to take advantage of strategic opportunities. It can also give competitors time to make successful preemptive moves.

Today some advanced users of computers are experiencing the pain of large conversions to new systems and vendors with which they can grow. Such customers are willing to undergo the immediate switching costs because of the benefits they will gain from being up-to-date in a product area that is growing in strategic importance.

Marketplace dynamics

A customer's position on the behavior spectrum does not remain constant over time, of course, especially in dynamic marketplaces. Changes occur because of environmental fluctuations, competitors' actions, other customer changes, sellers' actions, or simply because of the passage of time.

The computer marketplace provides an example of behavior change in process. One important force has been the movement toward what is called "network architecture" in large computer systems, with explicit rules for interfacing different parts of a system, facilitating the use within a single network of individual parts of different types, often from different vendors. In comparable fashion, conventions for interfacing can facilitate the use of software packages from different sources. It is becoming easier to mix and match components from different vendors or different components from the same vendor.

My field investigation shows that large computer system users are well aware of these networking effects. They have welcomed the change, sensing that it gives them bargaining power with suppliers and access to the innovations of more than one marketer.

Customers are making strong lost-for-good commitments to the technology of the lead vendor that determines the backbone or underlying network design. At the same time, however, customers are beginning to show always-a-share behavior in their purchases of individual hardware and software items.

A computer seller in the 1980s cannot assume that a customer is either totally committed or totally lost for the future, though such an assumption would have been reasonable in the 1960s. In the 1980s, customers' choices of their lead vendors and basic technology have been made with long time horizons and have emphasized long-term concerns and capabilities. At the same time, however, even marketers that won commitments as lead vendors have had to compete on short-term issues to win customers' patronage for components of the newer computer networks. Customers can view those individual purchases as separate transactions.

Vendor-induced changes

Other changes along the behavior spectrum can be induced by actions of customers and/or vendors, such as the use of formal procedures to create buying systems for customers and suppliers. Such systems provide efficiencies and improved service for the customer. They also create stronger links between the two organizations and raise the costs of switching suppliers.

American Hospital Supply's ASAP system demonstrates a strong bond between a vendor and its customers. The ASAP system allows customers to place orders for supplies and equipment easily and efficiently. For example, customers can order via a computer terminal, use standing or repetitive order files (to avoid retyping regularly ordered lists of products), and obtain order confirmations on their own tailored forms. The most advanced ASAP systems provide computer-to-computer links between the vendor and the hospital's materials management computer program; the customer's computer can automatically order needed items from the vendor without any human intervention.

While one might expect hospitals to show always-a-share behavior in purchasing such items as syringes and hospital gowns, the ASAP system has moved its customers close to the lost-for-good end of the spectrum. Customers buy groups of products as a system; they lose efficiency and convenience when they mix and match.[1]

In the example at the beginning of this article, Superior Shipping's sales force was trying to help customers plan their logistics. Superior might be able to help customers set up procedures that link them more closely to the seller, using information exchanged between buyer and seller that will facilitate efficient service. Superior might in this way offer improved service if customers involve Superior more closely in their scheduling procedures. If Superior's customers could be induced to make such investments in procedures, their behavior would move toward the lost-for-good end of the spectrum and Superior might then find it worthwhile to invest in helping customers plan and improve. (If Dale Spencer had done some of these things, perhaps he might have succeeded at Superior.)

In other cases, vendors can raise customer switching costs and move accounts closer to the lost-for-good model by offering system benefits—

additional real benefits that customers can obtain if they source more (or all) of their purchases from a single vendor. For example, a chemical company offers auto body shops access to a computer program for matching colors; the program translates information about a car's original color, age, condition, and other factors into instructions for using the vendor's pigments to match the car's current color for touch-ups and repairs. The program uses only the vendor's set of pigments; customers cannot easily mix and match.

Likewise, potential customers for private branch communication exchanges are urged to buy whole PBX systems from one vendor to obtain full software compatibility among individual products. For example, some procedures for reducing costs of long-distance calls and future electronic mail systems will depend on such compatibility.

In other situations, actions by one vendor can move another supplier's accounts closer to the always-a-share end of the spectrum, thus allowing the new vendor to enter the accounts. Product designs compatible with those of an established vendor can serve this purpose. Many suppliers of computer peripherals and software, for example, offer products that are compatible with IBM products; customers, therefore, can buy individual items that fit into an existing IBM system. Customers can experiment with new vendors in a limited way. In the process, they show behavior a little closer to the always-a-share model.

Vendors sometimes commit themselves to make their products work with those of other vendors. Lanier Business Products, for example, a supplier of individual devices for office automation, has advertised that its products will plug into (or work with) any of the emerging standards for networking such products together. Such accommodations allow customers to make purchase decisions without fear of locking themselves into a prescribed choice for their office networks.

Using the spectrum

Effective use of the behavior spectrum in marketing thus first involves analyzing patterns of customer behavior. It then calls for exploring possible actions by the vendor (or by the vendor's competitors) that can affect customers' positions along the spectrum. Here are some points to remember:

1   **To diagnose customers' behavior, analyze switching costs.**

What are the investments in dollars, people, lasting assets, or procedures required for the buyer to change? As noted, the larger and more disruptive the required investments, the closer the account will be to the lost-for-good end of the spectrum; the smaller the investments, the closer it will be to always-a-share.

What is the risk or exposure involved in changing? Will a difficult or unsuccessful change seriously hurt the customer's operations or the career of one of its managers? Such exposure will make the buyer more conservative, more reluctant to change.

What is the nature of the customer's usage system? Is it modular so that the buyer can try a new product in a reasonably isolated experiment? If so, the account can behave more like the always-a-share model. On the other hand, a closely integrated usage system that allows only substantial changes will produce behavior more like lost-for-good.

2   **To select a marketing approach, consider the position along the behavior spectrum.**

Use relationship marketing for buyers near the lost-for-good end of the spectrum. Purchasers of office automation systems or aircraft engines are apt examples.

Use transaction marketing for buyers near the always-a-share end of the spectrum, for example, purchasers of many commodity chemicals.

For customers in intermediate positions on the spectrum, use intermediate approaches. Such buyers will look beyond the immediate transaction but they will not have the long-term orientations of lost-for-good buyers.

3   **To analyze additional possible marketing actions, consider changes along the behavior spectrum.**

To move accounts closer to the lost-for-good end, build switching costs. Create systems that link the customers more closely to the vendor, for example, either through ordering systems or through procedures for delivery and inventory. Make it easier for the customer to do business with one supplier than with many. Or choose product designs that give customers substantial benefits from using a system of products from the same vendor.

To move accounts closer to always-a-share, give the buyers painless ways to mix and match. Sell products that fit into the customer's existing system built from other suppliers' products. Provide easy interfaces; give the customer assistance in making

1 For other such uses of information technology, see F. Warren McFarlan and James L. McKenney, *Corporate Information Systems Management: The Issues Facing Senior Executives* (Homewood, Ill.: Richard D. Irwin, 1983); see also James I. Cash and Benn R. Konsynski, "IS Redraws Competitive Boundaries," HBR March-April 1985, p. 134.

mixed usage systems work. Promise and deliver compatibility.

4   To use the concept of the spectrum successfully, consider the dimension of time.

Select a time horizon for evaluating marketing actions in light of the time horizons customers use in making commitments to suppliers. Obviously, don't make substantial up-front investments to win commitments that won't last. In addition, plan for and/or guard against preemptive moves that will affect customers' behavior along the spectrum. Successful competitive actions that move customers closer to the lost-for-good end can be extremely difficult to counter. Try to get there first.

Marketing challenge

The picture of long-term commitments from customers in the lost-for-good end of the behavior spectrum seems to be attractive in many ways. Close to the customer is good, isn't it? The answer to this question appears to be "yes, but." First, different degrees of closeness are possible in different situations; marketers should assess how much closeness is feasible. Also, my research indicates that building and maintaining strong, lasting customer ties (even where feasible) is a difficult marketing challenge.

Customers who are making strong commitments with long time horizons are concerned both with marketers' long-run capabilities and also with their immediate performance. Because the customers feel exposure, they especially demand vendor competence and commitment. They are likely to be frightened by even minor signs of supplier inadequacy.

As a result, successful relationship marketing involves doing a large number of things right, consistently, over time. It takes coordination on the part of the seller of resources and tools to meet the customer's future as well as its immediate needs.

The good news, therefore, is that (where feasible) strong, long-lasting relationships toward the lost-for-good end of the spectrum can be extremely attractive for marketers, whose actions can sometimes effectively encourage such behavior. The bad news — but also the opportunity — is that relationship marketing can be a difficult challenge for the marketer, often requiring up-front investment and consistently good performance on a variety of tasks. ▽

Bargaining by pantomime

The blue town, Tartary, is noted for its great trade in camels. The camel market is a large square in the center of the town. The animals are ranged here in long rows, their front feet raised upon a mud elevation constructed for that purpose, the object being to show off the size and height of the creatures. The uproar and confusion of this market are tremendous, with the incessant bawling of the buyers and sellers as they dispute, their chattering after they have agreed, and the horrible shrieking of the animals at having their noses pulled, for the purpose of making them show their agility in kneeling and rising....

The trade in camels is entirely by proxy — the seller and the buyer never settle the matter between themselves. They select indifferent persons to sell their goods, who propose, discuss, and fix the price; the one looking to the interest of the seller, the other to those of the purchaser. These 'sale speakers' exercise no other trade; they go from market to market, to promote business, as they say. They have generally a great knowledge of cattle, have much fluency of tongue, and are, above all, endowed with a knavery beyond all shame. They dispute by turns, furiously and argumentatively, as to the merits and defects of the animal; but as soon as it comes to a question of price, the tongue is laid aside as a medium, and the conversation proceeds altogether in signs. They seize each other by the wrist, and beneath the long, wide sleeves of their jackets indicate with their fingers the progress of the bargain. After the affair is concluded, they partake of the dinner, which is always given by the purchaser, and then receive a certain number of sapeks, according to the custom of the different places.

From
"Bargaining by Pantomime —
Trade in Camels"
in Frazar Kirkland
(pseudonym for
Richard Miller Devens)
*Cyclopaedia of Commercial
and Business Anecdotes,*
D. Appleton and Company,
New York, 1865, vol. 2, p. 603.

Reprint 85608

At Mackay Envelope Corporation, "know your customer" isn't a cliché, it's the foundation of the business.

Humanize Your Selling Strategy

by HARVEY B. MACKAY

You are sitting in a conference room with your marketing manager and sales staff, engaged in reviewing the account of a key customer. To begin her analysis, the account executive opens up the file folder and reads aloud:

"Staunch Republican"

"Midwestern value system"

"Enthusiastic booster of the Boy Scouts"

"Avid stamp collector"

"Procrastinates on major buying decisions...needs strong follow-through"

Of course, the report also includes data on the market position, new product lines, and plans for factory construction of the customer's company. But a sizable portion of the discussion focuses on the customer's personal chemistry and characteristics...and how well the salesperson understands these traits and creatively markets to them. Sound like a peculiar use of management time? For many marketers such a dis-

cussion would border on the unorthodox, but companies that ignore such vital and revealing information are at a distinct disadvantage in the marketplace.

Many companies are becoming ever more adept at using segmented marketing strategies. In mere seconds, video and print messages can establish instant rapport with a targeted customer. But in the meantime, businesses have lost sight of the need to humanize their selling strategies. Computerized purchase orders, rampant cost analysis, and sophisticated financial modeling have overwhelmed the salesperson-corporate customer relationship.

Envelopes are not a glamorous business. In fact, they are about as drab a commodity as you can imagine – in what is nearly the textbook definition of a mature industry. That means you have to be especially good at differentiating your company if you expect to gain market share. In the enve-

lope industry, Mackay's products are constantly being assaulted by newer, sexier, more convenient ways to communicate, like telephones and computers and electronic mail. A company's margins can be paper thin.

Despite these drawbacks, in the past five years Mackay Envelope has seen its sales volume rise an average 18% a year to $35 million, and its market share rise to 2% nationally (pretty good in this fragmented industry; there are 235 envelope companies in the country). Mackay has also become one of the most profitable companies in the industry. We credit our success to one factor more than any other: salesmanship – inspired, energized, superior salesmanship.

For years it was fashionable for U.S. executives with any decent pedigree to sneer at sales, the land of Willy Loman. But today we are beginning to see a mighty redirection of the resources of the American corporation. Head counts in administration, production, and R&D are dwindling, but sales forces are on the rise. When IBM announced it would trim its staff by 12,000 by the end of 1987, it simultaneously reassigned 3,000 people to its sales force. The transformation of Campbell Soup from a gray lady to a leading business innovator is largely attributed to a new marketing strategy that has focused on targeting and selling to sharply defined customer niches. Former Porsche CEO Peter Schutz, in an interview in this publication two years ago, stressed how much time he spent in the Porsche delivery room talking with customers and learning

Harvey B. Mackay is chairman of the board, chief executive officer, and sole owner of the Mackay Envelope Corporation, Minneapolis. William Morrow has just published his book Swim With the Sharks Without Being Eaten Alive.

about their motivations and idio-syncracies.[1]

At Mackay Envelope we use every means we can think of to exalt selling and salespeople. The parking place just outside the door of the main office is not reserved for the CEO. Above it is this sign:

Reserved for
[we fill in the name]
Salesperson of the Month.

This is our way of declaring to our 350 employees, our visitors, and the world at large that sales are at the very heart of our business.

During speaking engagements at management seminars from Athens to New Delhi, I have talked with operators of myriad other businesses, from truffles and textiles to trucks and high technology. The problems and challenges I have heard described are extraordinarily similar, and most of them turn on a failure to manage selling fundamentals. Use of a few simple tactics and disciplines can alleviate many problems.

Know your customer... in spades

In a one-hour lunch you can learn everything from a golf handicap to views on the federal deficit, from size of home to favorite vacation spot. "So what?" I've heard people say. "It's hard enough to remember my sales and inventory turnover from last month. Why should I clutter my brain and my files with this new version of Trivial Pursuit?" Because it establishes you as an effective listener, that's why. Effective listeners remember order dates and quality specifications. They are easier to talk with when there's a problem with a shipment. In short, effective listeners sell more customers...and keep them longer.

1. David E. Gumpert, "Porsche on Nichemanship," HBR March-April 1986, p. 98.

For 27 years at Mackay, we have used a device to get people to record and review this kind of data. It's a questionnaire form. People inside our company have taken to calling it the "Mackay 66" (because it has 66 questions). We complete at least one on every customer. It lists all the vital statistics we gather, such as our contact's educational background, career history, family, special interests, and life-style. It's continually updated and it's studied to death in our company. Our overriding goal is to know more about our customers than they know about themselves.

I've had people ask me, "Don't you feel like the FBI or the KGB, running dossiers on your customers?" I don't. The questionnaire is merely a system for organizing what the best executives and salespeople have done for a long time: demonstrate exceptional understanding of their customers as people.

The point here is that people don't truly care how much you know until they know how much you care. One purpose of the Mackay 66 is to empower the perceptive and empathetic salesperson with information that, channeled properly, produces a response that says "I care."

For example, question number 48 asks about the customer's vacation habits. These say a lot about people. Is he the outdoors type who loves to white-water raft on the Colorado or camp out at Yosemite? Does she like to tour Europe and Japan by bus? Is she a tennis enthusiast who plans her vacations around major professional tournaments?

How would that lover of the outdoors react to a book of photographs of Yosemite by Ansel Adams? What would the sightseeing type say on receiving an array of hard-to-get brochures of unusual and exotic tours? Imagine

the reaction of that tennis buff as she reads previews of Wimbledon and the U.S. Open we sent her a few weeks before those events.

Each of these instances happened. The donor wasn't a husband, wife, friend, or neighbor but a Mackay account executive. Were these gestures perceived as insincere? They could have been, but they weren't. They represented actions taken after seller

> ## People don't care how much you know until they know how much you care.

and buyer had achieved a certain level of communication and rapport. The best salespeople are "other conscious." They're sensitive people who are genuinely interested in others. They don't do things *to* people; they do things *for* people, after they've learned something about those people.

Who were the sources of information regarding the vacation habits? They could have been secretaries, receptionists, or other suppliers. They often are. In these situations, however, they were the prospective customers themselves. The information about vacations was cross-referenced to question number 51, "conversational interests." In each instance, this information was culled from the customer over breakfast or lunch (naturally, after the name of the customer's favorite restaurant was elicited from the secretary).

When the little gift came, it arrived on the prospective customer's birthday (the date is asked in question number 5), long after that introductory lunch or breakfast. Was the customer aware that the giver had an ulterior motive? Yes, in part. But what also came

CONTEMPLATED MERGERS:
EXXON/CAMPBELL'S

REGULAR   UNLEADED   CHICKEN GUMBO

across was the salesperson's thoughtfulness and sincere desire to establish a solid, long-term relationship. The personal touch is so rare a commodity today, it becomes a standout. Does it always translate into new business? Not always, but often; and not always immediately, but eventually.

I learned the impact of using one's intelligence on customers when, as a young constituent, I walked into Senator Hubert Humphrey's Washington office for the first time and he amazed me by showing he knew about my goals and avocations. Although we had only a brief conversation, his genuine likability and superior information turned me into a friend, a supporter, and a loyal contributor. The intent is not to get something on somebody. The goal is to pay attention to the *person* across the table. Salespeople sell to people, not computer terminals. I have found that salespeople who can't understand and empathize with the goals of the

people they sell to are incapable of understanding and empathizing with the goals of the broader organization they later have to serve in filling the order.

At any big social function you see effective top executives creating mental profiles on the people they meet. Leaders learn to pay attention to what's important in other people's lives. That means keeping your antennae up and noticing the details. It's not manipulation but disarmament. All of us are naturally hostile to persuasion and salesmanship. Well, everyone whose livelihood relies on making a sale had better learn to neutralize that hostility, so he or she can get on with the business of honestly selling the product. Our format simplifies the method and puts it into the hands of the little guy. With practice and a modicum of discipline, anyone can master the skill of harvesting customer awareness.

Once each year, our marketing people and our top operating

people sit down and review the material on our key customers, with special emphasis on the last page – the page that deals with the customer's view of the goals and issues facing that company's management, as stated to our salespeople. This analysis of common customer issues is the launching pad for our planning.

When a salesperson quits or retires, it is very difficult to sustain valuable personal relationships in business-to-business selling. But these continually updated files have allowed us to put a new client contact into position far faster than most businesses can. The greatest danger when you lose a veteran salesperson is, of course, that the client will be spirited away too. The documentation that the salesperson has built up (often over years) gives us a big edge in establishing a lasting relationship between the new Mackay account representative and the customer.

Ask the salespeople in any company, "Are you dealing with the same purchasing agent at Jones & Smith today as you were five years ago?" The answer is quite probably no. In international businesses especially, purchasing people are transferred often. Therefore, make a point of getting to know the whole department – especially the up-and-comers – and learn the company's practices on moving people. In short, dig your well before you're thirsty.

As a manager, I judge the intensity and the discipline of our 20-plus salespeople by looking at how up-to-date their customer profiles are. Scanning the profile is stage one of any account review. Sometimes a superficially completed profile or one filled with awkward hedges is a godsend of an early warning. It can signal a salesperson mismatch with an account. And *that* means a switch in account assignments before the customer decides to take a hike.

As important as the questionnaire is, it's vital not to confuse the form with the mind-set and discipline it represents. The form is just a tool to readjust people's vision. You and I have both sat across the table from too many salespeople whose eyes became glazed over with indifference, whose sighs of boredom betrayed their thought, which was: "Just sign the order, you're wasting my time"—as if you, the customer, were obligated to help boost the caller's profits. The method built around the questionnaire arms the seller with superior information and intelligence and inspires a positive attitude toward making the sale.

A salesperson never has to make a cold call. Ever. Granted

> The customer relationship is like a marriage—small shows of sensitivity and awareness maintain spice.

you aren't likely to learn much about family background and career history until you actually have your first meeting, but there is no reason you can't become an instant expert on a prospect company in advance. If it's a public company, your broker can round up an annual report and may be able to offer valuable insights too. I own at least one share of stock in every publicly traded company that is a customer. The public library is a powerful information arsenal, with countless business periodicals and readers' guides for tracking articles down. D&B reports are readily available and

highly informative, but I think their existence must be "one of the best kept secrets" in U.S. business. The prospect's own customers, its other suppliers, and even former employees all can be fertile sources.

Ask your friendly banker. "Isn't that breaching a confidence?" you ask. Not if your banker doesn't happen to be your customer's banker too. Then there's the chamber of commerce buyer's guide. (Every chamber has one.) You can even subscribe to a clipping service to monitor the local and trade press. The list of easily available background sources is nearly endless.

This research requires the same skills that went into writing a good term paper. But so few people think of applying these disciplines in a sales situation. So many people close the door on their education and training and don't even think of using in real life what they spent dozens of years learning. The best business recruits recognize that their real education doesn't begin until they enter the workplace—because then education becomes application. I constantly remind my people that knowledge doesn't become power until it's used. That's why we use the "Mackay 66." That's why we write it all down.

In 33 years of selling, I have never called on a buyer I haven't sold. In that I'm not exceptional. The diligence and perseverance of our company's selling strategy are, however, unusual. Hardly anyone ever makes a sale on the first call. That's just as true for us as anyone else. Not every lead qualifies as a legitimate prospect. But when we decide that we want a company's envelope business, we've ultimately made the sale in virtually every case.

Years ago, as the business was building, I (as CEO) made the first

call on most major prospects, and that call was invariably brief. I asked for 300 seconds of my counterpart's time, and usually the meeting lasted no more than 180 seconds. "We very much want to be your supplier," I'd say. "It means a lot to us. Here's what we can do...." My comments were confined to differentiators like price, quality, service, or delivery time—whatever distinguished us from the competing supplier.

Courtship & marriage

Many CEOs were terrific salespeople at early stages of their careers. But too often, after being installed in carpeted corner offices at headquarters, they have allowed a distance to grow between themselves and the sales arena. Then the CEO's only selling involvement takes place behind closed doors, pitching the board on a strategic plan or the executive committee on a management succession scenario.

That's a big mistake. Salespeople need to see the top people out there, mixing it up, setting the example. That's a prime reason why some of America's most visible chief executives, the Frank Perdues and Victor Kiams and Lee Iacoccas, are so effective when they get out in public to pitch their products on national television. They're not just selling products. They're also motivating their people to sell the products. Selling chickens may not be the most pleasant job in the world, but if the boss thinks it's important enough to do himself, then maybe it's important for the chicken salesperson too.

Most initial contacts are lengthy presentations with glowing claims concocted for audiences that are often too large and too highly placed. They abuse the customer's time. You don't need a Wagnerian epic to communicate a persuasive message. After all, the

Gettysburg Address has only 270 words and the Lord's Prayer, a mere 54.

The follow-up happens on the technical level. What the CEO as salesperson should be selling is not product. It is a strategic idea ...and it is trust.

The relationship is just like a marriage: small shows of sensitivity and awareness keep the spice in it. We have one customer whose version of heaven is salmon fishing in Scotland. You can bet that at least once a year an article on salmon angling from a fine British sporting magazine shows up on his desk, together with a handwritten note. A prospective customer, whom we have pursued for a year and a half, makes a pilgrimage to New York twice a year to feast on operas and concerts. Each September this client receives, in a Mackay envelope, the Carnegie Hall and Lincoln Center season programs. The personal touch is noticeably changing his attitude toward us.

We have a customer who is a University of Michigan alumnus

and a passionate Wolverine football fan. In 1986, Michigan won the Big Ten football title. My secretary found out where Rose Bowl programs were being printed, ordered a copy, and had it sent to him. He was unable to attend the game on New Year's Day, but I'm sure he sat in front of his living room TV with that program clutched in his hands.

It takes time. Strategic, humanized selling always does. It is also based on very self-evident precepts...astonishingly simple. As the Prussian strategist Karl von Clausewitz wrote in *On War*: "Everything in strategy is very simple, but that does not mean everything is very easy."

Care & feeding of salespeople

The stereotype of the huckster who cajoles his mark into resigned submission—that portrait is one for the business history books. Today's seller must understand modern communication styles and concepts. That begins with knowing when to close one's

mouth and open one's ears, but it entails a whole lot more.

Before we hire a salesperson, I always socialize with the candidate and the spouse. Too many important deals are secured in a social setting, like the ballpark or the ballet, for ease in handling contacts to be ignored. It's also important to see a candidate in his or her home setting. Is what you find at all like what you were told it would be? That is, is this person a straight shooter or prone to exaggeration? You don't want to learn later that a decade-long customer has been victimized by overpromises. I make a point of having a long telephone conversation with the candidate and sprinkling it with awkward pauses just to see how he or she handles them. Given the amount of business transacted by phone these days, you had better find out if you're signing up Ted Koppel or Archie Bunker.

We send our salespeople through Dale Carnegie or Toastmasters training because these courses emphasize how important listening is to effective speaking. Any outstanding public speaker will tell you that a speech is nothing more or less than the sale of an idea. The best speakers anchor their skills by monitoring audience feedback, from body language to the cough count.

Our constant exposure to electronic media has changed the way we expect to be persuaded. Persuaders must get to the point faster, speak in a vivid and engaging way, and blend their pitches so cleverly with customized information that it never sounds like mere patter.

An entire industry, insurance, has been built on the Law of Large Numbers. There are 264 million living Americans. The insurance people can predict within one-fourth of 1% how many of us will die within the next 12 months.

They can tell us where, and how, in what age bracket, and of what sex, race, and profession. The only thing they can't predict is who. The sales force must apply this same principle to its prospect lists. If the lists are long enough, there will be salespeople for Number One suppliers who retire or die, or lose their territories for a hundred other reasons.

What you can't predict is which of your competitors will succumb to the Law of Large Numbers. But fortunately, as in the insurance business, which one doesn't matter. All that matters is that your salespeople have the perseverance and patience to position your company as Number Two to enough prospects. If they're standing second in line in enough lines, sooner or later they will move up to Number One.

In our company, we recognize that the kind of dogged persistence and patience it takes to convert a Number Two position to a Number One position is very tough for the typical salesperson to master. By nature, salespeople tend to be more like racehorses than plowhorses. The instant gratification syndrome that gets a salesperson to the finish line first is an ingrained part of the salesperson's makeup. That's why we insist on the customer profiles, the follow-ups, the disciplined account review, and, most of all, the emphasis on human sensitivity. Doubtless, it is not the fanciest marketing management system, but it is uncommonly effective for managing salespeople.

Let me illustrate by passing on a conversation I had with a young salesperson named Phil (I'll call him). It was like a lot of talks I've had with my salespeople over the years. Phil came into my office looking agitated.

Phil. Mr. Mackay, I need your help. I've been wrestling for over a year now to get the account at International Transom, and it's just no use. I think I'd better give up.

Mackay (*motions him toward a chair*). They buy from Enveloping Envelope, don't they?

Phil (*sits*). Yes, for seven years, and they don't have the slightest interest in changing suppliers. I think it's time for me to write

> By making ourselves Number Two in many places, sooner or later we'll be Number One in some.

off this particular prospect and spend my time on business with greater promise.

Mackay. International Transom is a very attractive account, Phil. I wonder if you're not chasing the wrong goal. Accept for now that they're happy with EE. Your objective isn't to become their supplier overnight; it's to become the undisputed holder of second place. (*Phil looks skeptical, so Mackay proceeds to explain the Law of Large Numbers.*)

Phil (*gloomily*). Based on what I've seen in calling on Bystrom, the purchasing agent at International Transom, it's going to be a long wait.

Mackay. I see you've got the customer profile there. Let me take a look. (*Phil hands him the folder. Mackay reads it.*) Aha. Just as I thought. This questionnaire reads like a dry and pretty spotty profile on someone you find intimidating, if not a little hostile. There's no vitality, no real grasp of the customer or his motivation. It's lifeless.

Phil (*agitated again*). But this guy is a clam, not at all outgoing.

Mackay (*sternly*). Did you read his desk? Were there any mementos there that told you something about him? How about plaques on the wall? What's his alma mater? If he's businesslike with you, what are his aspirations? How does he identify with company goals? You don't have in here a recent article or current analyst's report on this company. (*Arises from his desk and gesticulates as he paces to and fro.*) How well have you shown him that you know and admire his company? That you know how it fits in its industry? Do you know the strengths and weaknesses of Enveloping Envelope in terms of International Transom? Have you emphasized to Bystrom those strengths that Mackay has almost exclusively, like centralized imprinting?

Phil. Well, I....

Mackay. Have you, in short, made Bystrom feel absolutely terrible about not buying from you right now? Terrible because you are so knowledgeable, aware, interested in him as a person, and representing a company that is clearly differentiated from EE in important and positive ways?

Phil (*looking more excited now than upset*). I see what you mean, Mr. Mackay. You're asking me to aspire to the Number Two position, if we can't be first. Instead of telling me to win, you're telling me to prepare to win.

Mackay (*patting Phil on the back as they move toward the office door*). Exactly, Phil. (*He beams at Phil.*) You've got the right idea.

It wasn't long before Phil's folder on his prospect sharpened and fattened considerably. In this he had a lot of help, by the way, from others at Mackay Envelope who knew International Transom, Bystrom, and Enveloping Envelope. We have a reward system that recognizes outstanding individual performers and reinforces collaborative behavior. We don't focus on just the top salesperson. Each month we also reward the best networking that leads to a sale. We recognize a salesperson whose persistence has paid off with substantial new business. We spotlight a salesperson whose customer or competitive insight produced a significant change in the way we do business.

Your selling strategy

My definition of a great salesperson is not someone who can get the order. Anyone can get the order if he or she is willing to make enough promises about price or delivery time or service. A great salesperson is someone who can get the order – and the reorder – from a prospect who is already doing business with someone else. No salespeople can aspire to that kind of selling unless they are prepared to think strategically and humanistically about their customers. The beauty of it is, though, that with patience and some simple tools, you don't have to be a strategic genius or a management psychologist to excel.

If, however, you are a CEO or a manager who determines the climate and attitudes in your company, then I counsel you strongly to ensure that selling and salespeople in your organization get proper leadership and the recognition they deserve. No matter how many strides you make in product quality or asset management or new design features, there is no tool more likely to harm or help your market share than your selling strategy. This is a lesson companies can learn on their own initiative...or, I have no doubt, they will learn at the hands of their competitors.

Reprint 88208

IDEAS FOR ACTION

Eight ways to save a disintegrating sale

Negotiating with a Customer You Can't Afford to Lose

by Thomas C. Keiser

"I like your product, but your price is way out of line. We're used to paying half that much!"

"Acme's going to throw in the service contract for nothing. If you can't match that, you're not even in the running."

"Frankly, I think we've worked out a pretty good deal here, but now you've got to meet my boss. If you thought I was tough..."

"Tell you what: If you can drop the price by 20%, I'll give you the business. Once you're in our division, you know, you'll have a lock on the whole company. The volume will be huge!"

"I can't even talk to you about payment schedule. Company policy is ironclad on that point."

"Look here, at *that* price, you're just wasting my time! I thought this was a serious bid! Who do you think you're talking to, some green kid?"

This wasn't supposed to happen. You've invested a lot of time earning a customer's trust and goodwill.

Thomas C. Keiser is senior vice president of the Forum Corporation, a training-and-education consulting firm in Boston.

You've done needs-satisfaction selling, relationship selling, consultative selling, customer-oriented selling; you've been persuasive and good-humored. But as you approach the close, your good friend the customer suddenly turns into Attila the Hun, demanding a better deal, eager to plunder your company's margin and ride away with the profits. You're left with a lousy choice: do the business unprofitably or don't do the business at all.

This kind of dilemma is nothing new, of course. Deals fall through every day. But businesses that depend on long-term customer relationships have a particular need to avoid win-lose situations, since backing out of a bad deal can cost a lot of future deals as well. Some buyers resort to hardball tactics even when the salesperson has done a consummate job of selling. The premise is that it costs nothing to ask for a concession. Sellers can always say no. They will still do the deal. But many sellers— especially inexperienced ones—say yes to even the most outrageous customer demands. Shrewd buyers can lure even seasoned salespeople into deals based on emotion rather than on solid business sense. So how do

you protect your own interests, save the sale, and preserve the relationship when the customer is trying to eat your lunch?

Joining battle is not the solution unless you're the only source of whatever the customer needs. (And in that case you'd better be sure you never lose your monopoly.) Leaving the field is an even worse tactic, however tempting it is to walk away from a really unreasonable customer.

Surprisingly, accommodation and compromise are not the answers either. Often a 10% price discount will make a trivial difference in the commission, so the salesperson quickly concedes it. But besides reducing your company's margin significantly, this kind of easy accommodation encourages the customer to expect something for nothing in future negotiations.

Compromise—splitting the difference, meeting the customer halfway—may save time, but because it fails to meet the needs of either party fully it is not the proverbial win-win solution. A competitor who finds a creative way to satisfy both parties can steal the business.

The best response to aggressive but important customers is a kind of

> # What do you do when your customer turns into Attila the Hun?

assertive pacifism. Refuse to fight, but refuse to let the customer take advantage of you. Don't cave in, just don't counterattack. Duck, dodge, parry, but hold your ground. Never close a door; keep opening new ones. Try to draw the customer into a creative partnership where the two of you work together for inventive solutions that never occurred to any of your competitors.

There are eight key strategies for moving a customer out of a hardball mentality and into a more productive frame of mind.

1. *Prepare by knowing your walk-away and by building the number of variables you can work with during the negotiation.* Everyone agrees about the walkaway. Whether you're negotiating an arms deal with the Russians, a labor agreement with the UAW, or a contract you can't afford to lose, you need to have a walk-away: a combination of price, terms, and deliverables that represents the least you will accept. Without one, you have no negotiating road map.

Increasing the number of variables is even more important. The more variables you have to work with, the more options you have to offer; the greater your options, the better your chances of closing the deal. With an important customer, your first priority is to avoid take-it-or-leave-it situations and keep the negotiation going long enough to find a workable deal. Too many salespeople think their only variable is price, but such narrow thinking can be the kiss of death. After all, price is one area where the customer's and the supplier's interests are bound to be at odds. Focusing on price can only increase animosity, reduce margin, or both.

Instead, focus on variables where the customer's interests and your own have more in common. For example, a salesperson for a consumer-goods manufacturer might talk to the retailer about more effective ways to use advertising dollars—the retailer's as well as the manufacturer's—to promote the product. By including marketing programs in the discussion, the salesperson helps to build value into the price, which will come up later in the negotiation.

The salesperson's job is to find the specific package of products and services that most effectively increases value for the customer without sacrificing the seller's profit. For example, an automotive parts supplier built up its research and development capacity, giving customers the choice of doing their own R&D in-house or farming it out to the parts supplier. Having this option enabled the supplier to redirect negotiations away from price and toward creation of value in the product-development process. Its revenues and margins improved significantly.

Even with undifferentiated products, you can increase variables by focusing on services. A commodity chemicals salesperson, for example, routinely considered payment options, quantity discounts, bundling with other purchases, even the relative costs and benefits of using the supplier's tank cars or the customer's. Regardless of industry, the more variables you have, the greater your chances of success.

2. *When under attack, listen.* Collect as much information as possible from the customer. Once customers have locked into a position, it is difficult to move them with arguments, however brilliant. Under these circumstances, persuasion is more a function of listening.

Here's an example from my own company. During a protracted negotiation for a large training and development contract, the customer kept trying to drive down the per diem price of our professional seminar leaders. He pleaded poverty, cheaper competition, and company policy. The contract was a big one, but we were already operating at near capacity, so we had little incentive to shave the per diem even slightly. However, we were also selling books to each seminar participant, and that business was at least as important to us as the services. The customer was not asking for concessions on books. He was only thinking of the per diem, and he was beginning to dig in his heels.

At this point our salesperson stopped talking, except to ask questions, and began listening. She learned a great deal—and uncovered an issue more important to the customer than price.

The customer was director of T&D for a large corporation and a man with career ambitions. To get the promotion he wanted, he needed visibility with his superiors. He was afraid that our professionals would develop their own relationships with his company's top management, leaving him out of the loop. Our salesperson decided to give him the control he wanted. Normally we would have hired free-lancers to fill the gap between our own available

staff and the customer's needs. But in this case she told him he could hire the free-lancers himself, subject to our training and direction. The people we already employed would be billed at their full per diem. He would save money on the free-lancers he paid directly, without our margin. We would still make our profit on the books and the professional services we did provide. He would maintain control.

Moreover, we were confident that the customer was underestimating the difficulty of hiring, training, and managing free-lancers. We took the risk that somewhere down the road

When customers attack, keep them talking.

the customer would value this service and be willing to pay for it. Our judgment turned out to be accurate. Within a year we had obtained the entire professional services contract without sacrificing margin.

It was a solution no competitor could match because no competitor had listened carefully enough to the customer's underlying agenda. Even more important, the buyer's wary gamesmanship turned to trust, and that trust shaped all our subsequent negotiations.

When under attack, most people's natural response is to defend themselves or to counterattack. For a salesperson in a negotiation, either of these will fuel an upward spiral of heated disagreement. The best response, however counterintuitive, is to keep the customer talking, and for three good reasons. First, new information can increase the room for movement and the number of variables. Second, listening without defending helps to defuse any anger. Third, if you're listening, you're not making concessions.

3. *Keep track of the issues requiring discussion.* Negotiations can get confusing. Customers often get frustrated by an apparent lack of progress; they occasionally go back on agreements already made; they

sometimes raise new issues at the last moment. One good way to avoid these problems is to summarize what's already been accomplished and sketch out what still needs to be discussed. Brief but frequent recaps actually help maintain momentum, and they reassure customers that you're listening to their arguments.

Piecemeal negotiating gives the hungry customer one slice at a time.

The best negotiators can neutralize even the most outspoken opposition by converting objections into issues that need to be addressed. The trick is to keep your cool, pay attention to the customer's words and tone, and wait patiently for a calm moment to summarize your progress.

4. *Assert your company's needs.* Effective salespeople always focus on their customers' interests—not their own. They learn to take on a customer perspective so completely that they project an uncanny understanding of the buyer's needs and wants. Too much empathy can work against salespeople, however, because sales bargaining requires a dual focus—on the customer and on the best interests of one's own company. The best negotiating stance is not a single-minded emphasis on customer satisfaction but a concentration on problem solving that seeks to satisfy both parties. Salespeople who fail to assert the needs of their own company are too likely to make unnecessary concessions.

The style of assertion is also extremely important. It must be nonprovocative. "You use our service center 50% more than our average customer. We've got to be paid for that…" will probably spark a defensive reaction from a combative customer. Instead, the salesperson should build common ground by emphasizing shared interests, avoiding inflammatory language, and encour-

aging discussion of disputed issues. This is a better approach: "It's clear that the service center is a critical piece of the overall package. Right now you're using it 50% more than our average customer, and that's driving up our costs and your price. Let's find a different way of working together to keep service costs down and still keep service quality high. To begin with, let's figure out what's behind these high service demands."

5. *Commit to a solution only after it's certain to work for both parties.* If a competitive customer senses that the salesperson is digging into a position, the chances of successfully closing the deal are dramatically reduced. A better approach is to suggest hypothetical solutions. Compare these two approaches in selling a commercial loan:

"I'll tell you what. If you give us all of the currency exchange business for your European branches, we'll cap this loan at prime plus one."

"You mentioned the currency exchange activity that comes out of your European branches. Suppose you placed that entirely with us. We may be able to give you a break in the pricing of the new loan."

The first is likely to draw a counterproposal from a competitive customer. It keeps the two of you on opposite sides of the negotiating table. The second invites the customer to help shape the proposal. Customers who participate in the search for solutions are much more likely to wind up with a deal they like.

Some salespeople make the mistake of agreeing definitively to an issue without making sure the overall deal still makes sense. This plays into the hands of an aggressive customer trying to get the whole loaf one slice at a time. It's difficult to take back a concession. Instead, wrap up issues tentatively. "We agree to do X, provided we can come up with a suitable agreement on Y and Z."

6. *Save the hardest issues for last.* When you have a lot of points to negotiate, don't start with the toughest, even though it may seem logical to begin with the deal killers. After all, why spend time on side is-

sues without knowing whether the thorniest questions can be resolved?

There are two reasons. First, resolving relatively easy issues creates momentum. Suppose you're working with a customer who's bound and determined to skin you alive when it comes to the main event. By starting with lesser contests and finding inventive solutions, you may get the customer to see the value of exploring new approaches. Second, discussing easier issues may uncover additional variables. These will be helpful when you finally get down to the heart of the negotiation.

7. *Start high and concede slowly.* Competitive customers want to see a return on their negotiation investment. When you know that a customer wants to barter, start off with something you can afford to lose. Obviously, game playing has its price. Not only do you train your customers to ask for concessions, you also teach them never to relax their guard on money matters. Still, when the customer really wants to wheel and deal, you have little choice.

The customer too can pay a price for playing games. A classic case involves a customer who always bragged about his poker winnings, presumably to intimidate salespeople before negotiations got started. "I always leave the table a winner," he seemed to be saying. "Say your prayers." What salespeople actually did was raise their prices 10% to 15% before sitting down to negotiate.

Some salespeople make their worst mistake before they ever sit down at the table.

They'd let him win a few dollars, praise his skill, then walk away with the order at a reasonable margin.

A number of studies have shown that high expectations produce the best negotiating results and low expectations the poorest. This is why salespeople must not let themselves be intimidated by the customer who

Two Common Mistakes

Combative buyers are hard enough to handle without provoking them further, yet many salespeople unintentionally annoy buyers to the point of complete exasperation. What's worse, the two most common mistakes crop up most frequently at times of disagreement, the very moment when poking sticks at the customer ought to be the last item on your list of priorities.

The first mistake is belaboring. Some salespeople will repeat a single point until customers begin to feel badgered or heckled. Chances are they heard you the first time. You can also belabor a customer with logic or with constant explanations that seem to suggest that the customer is none too bright.

The second mistake is rebutting every point your customer makes, which is almost certain to lead to an argument—point and counterpoint. Don't say "night" every time your customer says "day," even if you're convinced the customer is wrong.

always bargains every point. Once they lower their expectations, they have made the first concession in their own minds before the negotiation gets under way. The customer then gets to take these premature concessions along with the normal allotment to follow.

A man I used to know—the CEO of a company selling software to pharmacies—always insisted on absolute candor in all customer dealings. He'd begin negotiations by showing customers his price list and saying, "Here's our standard price list. But since you're a big chain, we'll give you a discount." He broke the ice with a concession no one had asked for and got his clock cleaned nearly every time.

The key is always to get something in return for concessions and to know their economic value. Remember that any concession is likely to have a different value for buyer and seller, so begin by giving things that the customer values highly but that have little incremental cost for your company:

Control of the process
Assurance of quality
Convenience
Preferred treatment in times of product scarcity
Information on new technology (for example, sharing R&D)
Credit
Timing of delivery
Customization
Service

There's an old saying, "He who concedes first, loses." This may be true in a hardball negotiation where the customer has no other potential source of supply. But in most competitive sales situations, the salesperson has to make the first concession in order to keep the deal alive. Concede in small increments, get something in return, and know the concession's value to both sides. Taking time may seem crazy to salespeople who have learned that time is money. But in a negotiation, *not* taking time is money.

8. *Don't be trapped by emotional blackmail.* Buyers sometimes use emotion—usually anger—to rattle salespeople into making concessions they wouldn't otherwise make. Some use anger as a premeditated tactic; others are really angry. It doesn't matter whether the emotion is genuine or counterfeit. What does matter is how salespeople react. How do you deal with a customer's rage and manage your own emotions at the same time?

Here are three different techniques that salespeople find useful in handling a customer who uses anger—wittingly or unwittingly—as a manipulative tactic.

☐ Withdraw. Ask for a recess, consult with the boss, or reschedule the meeting. A change in time and place can change the entire landscape of a negotiation.

Author's note: I wish to acknowledge the ideas of Ann Carol Brown, David Berlew, John Carlisle, Greg Crawford, Richard Pascale, Mike Pedler, Neil Rackham, and my colleagues at the Forum Corporation.

☐ Listen silently while the customer rants and raves. Don't nod your head or say "uh-huh." Maintain eye contact and a neutral expression, but do not reinforce the customer's behavior. When the tirade is over, suggest a constructive agenda.

☐ React openly to the customer's anger, say that you find it unproductive, and suggest focusing on a specific, nonemotional issue. There are two keys to this technique. The first is timing: don't rush the process or you risk backing the customer into a corner from which there is no graceful escape. The second is to insist that the use of manipulative tactics is unacceptable and then to suggest a constructive agenda. Don't be timid. The only way to pull this off is to be strong and assertive.

For example, imagine this response to a customer throwing a fit: "This attack is not constructive. [Strong eye contact, assertive tone.] We've spent three hours working the issues and trying to arrive at a fair and reasonable solution. Now I suggest that we go back to the question of payment terms and see if we can finalize those."

Of course, there is substantial risk in using any of these techniques. If you withdraw, you may not get a second chance. If you listen silently or react ineffectively, you may alienate the customer further. These are techniques to resort to only when the discussion is in danger of going off the deep end, but at such moments they have saved many a negotiation that looked hopeless.

The essence of negotiating effectively with aggressive customers is to sidestep their attacks and convince them that a common effort at problem solving will be more profitable and productive. Your toughest customers will stop throwing punches if they never connect. Your most difficult buyer will brighten if you can make the process interesting and rewarding. The old toe-to-toe scuffle had its points, no doubt. Trading blow for blow was a fine test of stamina and guts. But it was no test at all of imagination. In dealing with tough customers, creativity is a better way of doing business. ▽

Reprint 88605

Gettings Things Done

Customer-driven distribution systems

Louis W. Stern and Frederick D. Sturdivant

You design products for specific customer groups. Here's how to distribute them the same way.

Too often, distribution is the neglected side of marketing. Automobile companies, savvy in many aspects of strategy, have lost huge shares of the parts and service markets to NAPA, Midas, and Goodyear because they resist making changes in their dealer franchise networks. A great many other American companies—Tupperware springs to mind—are reaching their markets in similarly outmoded ways. It is hardly seemly for Tupperware to continue with its "parties" when more than half of American women are working outside their homes.

In contrast, a number of companies have outstripped their competition with imaginative strategies for getting products to their customers— and marketing executives can learn from them. The Federal Express system is so innovative and formidable that it might be considered a model even beyond the small-package delivery industry. American Hospital Supply has gained the edge over its competition by linking up to hospitals and clinics with a sophisticated system of data processing, while Steelcase has set a standard for delivering complex office furniture installations, complete and on time.

Although American companies have been ignoring the ways in which they deliver products and services, their customers are increasingly inclined to demand higher standards of performance. Customers want companies to value their time and trouble.

And so, important opportunities for gaining a competitive advantage through distribution remain, and given the new technology, some companies may, as Federal Express has, achieve a breakthrough. Will the management of American companies (deregulated telecommunications companies included) make use of these opportunities or even recognize them for what they are? Just what process should a company use to select or structure the best possible distribution channels for its products?

We suggest eight steps to design a distribution system that really performs. The word *process* is key here because whatever the result of taking these steps, management will gain by clarifying what its customers want and how to serve them. Managers are always saying that they want their company to be "market driven." In following these steps, they can give substance to what is too often merely corporate rhetoric.

Step 1: Find out what your customers want

Of all marketing decisions, the ones regarding distribution are the most far-reaching. A company can easily change its prices or its advertising. It can hire or fire a market research agency, revamp its sales promotion program, even modify its product line. But once a company sets up its distribution channels, it will generally find changing them to be difficult.

And so, the first step calls for researching what customers want from the buying process and then using their preferences to group customers into market segments. Managers conducting the research concentrate on learning what their ultimate customers—the end users—want in the way of service. It is these people, of course, who actually benefit from the products a company makes.

It is important for the researchers to emphasize that the product's quality is not an issue. Nor should there be any question at this stage of what may or may not be most practical for the company, whether a service

Louis Stern is the John D. Gray Distinguished Professor of Marketing at the J. L. Kellogg Graduate School of Management at Northwestern University. He is the coauthor (with Adel I. El-Ansary) of the textbook Marketing Channels *(Prentice-Hall, 1982) and has published scores of articles on marketing management and marketing channel relationships. In 1986, he won the Paul D. Converse award for outstanding contribution to theory and science in marketing, presented by the American Marketing Association.*

Frederick Sturdivant is senior vice president of The MAC Group, Inc. and head of its San Francisco office. He is the author of The Corporate Social Challenge: Cases & Commentaries *(3d ed., Richard D. Irwin, 1985) and of several other books on marketing and business strategy. Before joining The MAC Group, he was on the faculty of the Harvard Business School and held the M. Riklis Chair at Ohio State University.*

company, a manufacturer, or a middleman. Rather, respondents should be encouraged to consider the delivery of the service, the convenience of shopping for the product, and the kind of add-ons that are sold along with either.

There is, of course, no such thing as a truly homogeneous market, in which all customers view the company's offerings in exactly the same way. Yet managers who routinely try to ascertain what market segments are worth preparing for when they design a product rarely try this when they make decisions about how to distribute it. This is a crucial mistake.

The preliminary research is meant to generate an inventory of customers' desires, but it is important to exclude ideas too grand or trivial for consideration. Without restrictions of

THOMAS PICKETT, Brasier, (late Servant to Mr Hancock in Pall Mall) lives at the Sign of ye Frying-Pan, in Compton Street ye Corner of Frith Street John Maketh selleth & tinneth all Sorts of Brass Copper & Iron Houshold-Goods.

any kind, who wouldn't ask for the moon? Needless to say, an overarching consideration is price: respondents should be made to realize that for every service (or lack of one) there will be a correspondingly higher or lower price. Equally important, however, respondents must be forced to weigh their preferences not only in relation to price but also in relation to one another.

1 See Paul E. Green, "Hybrid Models of Conjoint Analysis: An Expository Review," *Journal of Marketing Research,* May 1984, p. 155.

Consider personal computers. The delivery of service might include such things as a demonstration of the product before sale or the provision of long-term warranties and flexible financing. After the sale, there might be training programs for using the equipment and a program to install and repair it. Customers might appreciate "loaners" while their equipment is being repaired or technical advice over a telephone hot line. They should be prepared to make trade-offs among these inducements.

Services, we've found, usually fall into five categories:

Lot size. Do customers want to buy in units of one or in multiple units?

Market decentralization. Do customers value around-the-corner convenience, or are they willing to deal across great distances, say via an 800 number?

Waiting time. Do customers want immediate delivery, or are they more concerned about the assurance of delivery?

Product variety. Do customers value having the choice of many related products, or do they prefer the store to specialize?

Service backup. Do customers want immediate, in-house repair and technical help, or can they wait and choose their own local repair services?

Once customers have traded off, say, demands for convenient location against product variety or variety against expert sales assistance, researchers can group these preferences into market segments and look for links between the segments suggested by the survey and the segments that may be generated by analysis of independent demographic or other marketing data.

We suspect, for example, that a segment of small businesses would be much more concerned about one-stop shopping than large businesses; big companies have purchasing specialists with the time to choose complementary products from different sources and to secure the lowest prices within various quality ranges. If a company sells to people who want one-stop shopping, it might want to know whether this segment coincides with self-employed accountants, for example. This

small market segment is likely to be substantial, and it has needs quite different from those of a segment consisting of start-up scientific research companies.

A number of marketing research techniques are available to researchers at this step in the process, among them conjoint analysis, hybrid modeling, and constant-sum scales.[1] Unfortunately, most of these techniques have been developed to elicit choices among the tangible properties of product design: gas mileage versus size of car, size versus model, and so on. The things people want from a distribution system tend to be less tangible and more difficult to visualize and make judgments about (convenience of location versus depth of assortment, for example). Survey instruments ought to be designed with this challenge in mind.

Step 2: Decide on appropriate outlets

At this stage researchers focus on the relation between market segments – defined as clusters of demands for service – and the outlets where services are normally delivered. Suppose, for example, that customers for a home computer indicate a desire for "self-service," "a somewhat narrow assortment of merchandise," "limited after-sale service," and "a relatively Spartan atmosphere" – so long as the prices are low. Clearly, this segment consists of people who would put up with a discount store operation – a 47 St. Photo, for instance – and trade off the amenities of upscale service or nearby location.

The fame of a store such as 47 St. Photo can be an asset in the analysis. Using the names of such well-known existing outlets or suggesting a hybrid of two or more kinds of such outlets, researchers can label potential clusters of service attributes. Respondents are asked about the service outlets they visualize, and researchers label the clusters constituting a segment precisely and vividly. On the other hand, labels are merely points of reference. They suggest existing kinds of retail outlets without limiting the possibilities.

For clusters suggesting no existing kinds of outlets, short descriptions of hypothetical outlets may be of help. Researchers may coin new names and, in analyzing the data, position the various segments along a wide continuum. The chemical industry, for example, may have no analog to a discount store or a rack jobber. But if many respondents indicate that they would like to see something along these lines, then the research team might, in the course of the survey, develop an appropriate option, describe it, think of a label for it, and present it to new respondents for consideration.

Venturesome financial institutions such as Merrill Lynch, Bank One, and GE Credit have scored impressive gains with just such distribution ideas. How else did we get to "financial supermarkets" and "discount brokerage"? In contrast, many marketing strategists in the personal computer industry have failed to predict the significance of value-added resellers or retail outlets with multiple but highly focused assortments. Obviously, they did not start by conceiving their distribution channels according to the shopping needs of potential customers.

Do not be hamstrung by industry experience. The more creative researchers are with their labels, the better step 2 will work.

Step 3:
Find out about the costs

Up to this point, the customer is sovereign: the process aims to determine what customers perceive to be optional shopping conditions among the many pertaining to distribution and related services. In the first part of step 3, however, it is essential to obtain an impartial assessment of whether the things that customers want (more precisely, the "clusters" of things they want) are feasible for the company. This is the first reality check, one that is made before management as a whole gets involved in the process.

It may be made by selected members of the corporation's staff, assuming they are professionals who can be objective about the company's line operations. Otherwise, the company must turn to executives from unaffected wholesaling or retailing enterprises or to academic authorities.

Researchers have already asked customers to trade off their demands for service against price, so that

utterly implausible combinations of shopping conditions – outlets combining small-lot purchases and low unit prices, for example – have been eliminated from further consideration. But less obviously implausible combinations may remain. Suppose a group of customers for personal computers claim they are willing to "pay any price" for a hypothetical shopping outlet combining custom tailoring with quick delivery. Are these two shopping conditions ever practical in combination?

The second part of step 3 aims to determine what kind of support will be needed from suppliers or other "up-channel" participants for any hypothetical outlet suggested by the data. Distribution outlets do not operate in isolation; there is always a distribution system backing them up.

For example, if an attribute cluster suggests a "limited line, full function, vertically oriented industrial distributor," the question would be this: What backup system ensures that this kind of distribution will satisfy customers as well as possible? The answers should be concrete: high-technology distribution centers, training programs, catalog expertise. Sometimes existing distribution systems enjoy the necessary support, sometimes not. If not, the division of labor among suppliers will have to be restructured so that what customers desire may be delivered by the most capable up-channel participant.

Step 3 is a good time to get insights from people out in the distributive trades. It is also the time to tap in-house knowledge, the opinions of salespersons and others who stay in contact with customers.

The third and final part of step 3 is to project the cost of support systems feasible for each outlet type, on the assumption that the company may be able to contract with third parties to perform the outlet functions. Researchers cost out the new support systems on an incremental basis, starting with the company's existing distribution system. Costing requires informed guesswork; any change in one element of a distribution system has ramifications for another. But if, for example, the data suggest that customers want rapid delivery, local inventories will have to be maintained. Distribution centers may have to be constructed to support the local inventories. Cost accountants familiar with distribution may provide estimates, although they may have trouble dealing with the more theoretical scenarios. In the end, the question to be answered is this: What increase in market share is required to offset the added costs of the new distribution alternatives?

It is important to collect these cost estimates during step 3 because they are backup material for step 4. The figures may well reveal that certain systems of distribution are prohibitively expensive and should be removed from further consideration. We know one manufacturer of specialty medical supplies and equipment that was losing sales to competitors selling via mail order. But the added cost of establishing a competing catalog system did not make sense, so the company abandoned the option at this stage.

Step 4:
Bound the 'ideal'

At this point the researchers have come as close as they can to discerning an ideal market-driven system.

Top management has been obliged to keep its hands off. Researchers have had a chance to find out, perhaps for the first time, what it really takes to please customers.

Step 4 gives a cross section of the company's executives an opportunity to subject the research findings to their own hard tests. Researchers invite these executives to investigate how any existing or hypothetical channel of distribution would affect company efficiency (costs, revenues, and profits), effectiveness (especially market share), and adaptability (fluidity of capital invested, ability to accept new products or adjust to new technologies). At the same time, executives give their impressions of what distribution is or is not doing. Though this part of the process is meant to generate reliable numbers, discussions with managers should be open-ended. They may even bring up their pet peeves.

Finally, researchers develop a list of company objectives for distribution based on their conversations with top management. They turn this list into a survey instrument and send it to every executive in the company who has a stake in distribution matters. Executives trade off objectives in the same way that customers trade off their requirements for outlet design. The result is a list of weighted objectives that are the constraints bounding the system.

Think of the 'ideal' distribution system. Then introduce reality.

Inevitably, at this stage, some executives want to impose constraints on the distribution design, which they justify not so much by numbers as by industrial tradition. There are rigidities and prejudices in most industries, some of which are reinforced by law, some of which are perceived to have the force of law.

The faltering car dealer system has not been altered for more than 60 years, in part because of peculiarities in the legal structure of auto distribution (franchise laws, dealer-day-in-

court laws). But there is also an industry folklore that gets in the way of change, even though auto companies face a shift in power to consolidating dealers. How much longer before the executives of Chrysler, GM, Toyota, and other companies will be forced to compare their old objectives with new options?

The Coca-Cola Company and PepsiCo, in contrast, are consolidating their traditionally independent franchise bottler networks into distribution systems with greater maneuverability. At IBM, distribution by means of a direct sales force had been a sacred principle essentially until the company started making personal computers. It finally began to use third parties but only after great internal strain, after which the personal computer division was accorded the status of an independent business unit.

Step 5: Compare your options

With the completion of step 4, company researchers will have a weighted list of management's objectives and constraints on the one hand and on the other a roster of the various ideal, market-driven distribution systems generated earlier in the process. Step 5 requires them to compare these two sets of data with each other and also with the system of distribution already in place. The researchers will, of course, consult with distribution managers about the company's present system: structure, functions performed by various channel participants, costs, discounts, and the like. It may be necessary for researchers to undertake an analysis of volume flows by channels as well as by margins, functions, and value-added at each level. A reasonably detailed map of this type can be very illuminating.

One of three conclusions will emerge from these comparisons. First, the existing system, the management-bounded system, and the ideal system may closely resemble each other. If this is the case, then management knows for sure that the existing system is about as good as it can get. If customer satis-

faction is mediocre nevertheless, the message should be clear: the fault lies not in the design of the system but in its implementation.

Second, the existing and management-bounded systems may be similar to each other but substantially different from the ideal. This outcome may mean that the objectives and constraints adopted by management are causing the gap. Such a finding calls for a careful investigation of management's perceptions, the purpose of step 6.

Third and especially sobering, all three systems may be substantially different. Assuming that the management-bounded system is positioned somewhere between the existing and the ideal, it may be possible to improve customer satisfaction without relaxing management's objectives. This is the time to ask if relaxation of certain management constraints might not produce even greater benefits.

By 1980, IBM's direct sales force and sales branches had formed the core of the distribution network for its existing line—mainframe and word processors. These channels could not, however, be cost-effective in delivering personal computers to the small business market—not, in any case, at the standard for customer satisfaction that IBM's executives considered their company's hallmark.

Iohn Wildblood at the Rainbow & 3 pidgons in St Clements Lane. In Lombard Street London who Married the Widdow Harrinton Silk Dyer

The ideal would have been a network of highly decentralized, service-intensive specialty stores carrying an assortment of personal computer brands and models as well as other types of office equipment. Because some IBM executives were convinced that the company could not maintain control over the quality of service without ownership, the company opened its own retail outlets to sell IBM equipment alone. IBM product centers offered the consumer a variety of equipment, but comparison shopping within them was impossible. In 1986, IBM sold off its product center network to NYNEX. (Interestingly enough, IBM has since come to realize that the small business market is so heterogeneous that it consists of multiple segments.)

And so the ideal system acts as a stake in the ground. If the management-bounded options are not reasonably similar to the ideal, then researchers will ultimately have to confront managers with the fact that the company has been sacrificing customer satisfaction to other objectives.

In the long run, some of these other objectives may be critical and may even supersede the effort to satisfy customers via distribution. When management decides on any new strategy, it will simultaneously establish a hurdle rate—a minimum projected return on investment that justifies going ahead. Managers may, of course, set hurdles incorrectly, not only because they miscalculate costs but because they acquire a prejudice for or against particular channels of distribution. In any case, distribution strategies that do not clear their hurdles should be dropped from consideration in step 5.

Step 6:
Review your pet assumptions

This step is meant to help distinguish a serious constraint from an ordinary prejudice. It entails bringing in outsiders—lawyers, political consultants, distribution experts from other industries—who will call management's assumptions into question. Management often protects the status quo, for example, by claiming that changes might violate the law or encourage shadowy activities. Outsiders can look at the relevant laws and ask if they are what they seem. Can't they be changed? Does holding to one value force the company to sacrifice another?

The automobile industry has clung steadfastly to the dealer franchise system, in part out of fear of legal tangles. Porsche's attempt to implement a more consumer-responsive approach to distribution in the early 1980s turned into a fiasco largely because Porsche's dealers made clear that it would keep the company tied up in the courts for a generation. Alas, Porsche was on the right track.

But the impulse to stand pat does not always stem from anxiety about the law. The use of authorized third-party outlets for personal computers is an example: it often portends gray market activities. Some time ago, top managers at IBM indicated that they had been worried about the price cutting and "footballing" that would result if they authorized third-party outlets—a concern that proved justified. Had they let this serious concern paralyze them, their personal computer division would never have expanded as quickly as it did.

And so during step 6, outside authorities should be called on to check whether legal and other constraints exist and, if they do, whether they can be overcome. Of course reliance on outside experts can be risky. Who is to say top management doesn't know what it is talking about? Who can tell what course a lawsuit will take or what laws Congress and state legislatures will enact?

Business decisions are based on judgments, not certainties. Merrill Lynch would never have launched its highly successful cash management account program if it had not altered its assumptions about how the SEC would enforce federal banking laws. What are other companies missing?

Step 7:
Confront the gap

This is the climax of the process. It requires top management to confront the gap between its practices or objectives and the ideal. For the first and only time, managers conducting the research bring together all executives responsible for distribution to determine the shape of a new system. To underline its significance, the company holds the meeting somewhere offsite.

The researchers get things going by presenting the ideal distribution system. Then they share the results of steps 4 and 5. In the course of this discussion, researchers outline for top management the objectives and constraints that were used to bound the ideal and show their effect, if any, in limiting what customers really desire. Next, researchers present the data and expert opinions challenging the validity of management's objectives and constraints—what was gained from step 6.

All this information serves as background for what usually proves to be a provocative discussion. We have found that researchers can prompt openness to it if they use computers to readjust weightings or other data and display the results instantaneously. This session brings top management

---

Sometimes the law prevents change. More often the obstacle is habit.

---

face-to-face with the folklore restricting its thinking. Executives compare alternatives, weigh opportunity costs in relation to risk and exposure, and consider a host of other quantitative and subjective variables that are all too easily buried under day-to-day affairs. Most important, they make decisions in a new context—one in which an attainable ideal has been delineated, the intervening distance between the ideal and the reality has been measured, and the obstacles to closing the gap have been made explicit.

Such was the case for a personal care products company, whose ideal suggested the elimination of one level in its system—the brokers. It was a big step for managers to contemplate. When the company's brand lacked visibility and strong consumer demand, brokers had played a key role in providing access to the retail trade. Management felt a strong sense of loyalty and indebtedness to them. Over the years the brand had emerged as the best seller in its category; now the brokers contributed little to volume. Indeed, a growing price sensitivity on the part of consumers, coupled with the inefficiency of the broker system, placed the manufacturer in a vulnerable position.

It's not important to know this company's final decision. What is important is how the process teased out the lines of a crucial choice. Apple Computer, for example, would not likely have experimented with mail order channels in its early history had it followed this line of investigation to its conclusion. It would have found that the amount of hand-holding required to make a personal computer plus a software sale is extremely high. Similarly, IBM would not have been so surprised to find that dealers with outbound sales forces have greater staying power than those who simply rely on inbound retail sales. IBM retail showrooms cannot provide the kind of indepth analysis and training that visits to a customer's premises can.

Step 8:
Prepare to implement

The final step in the process modifies the ideal distribution system emerging from step 3 according to the final objectives and constraints established in step 7. What managers are left with is a good system—not ideal, perhaps, but optimal.

This should be the subject of intensive implementation planning. And it is important for senior managers to help implement the system, if for no other reason than to give them a personal stake in the outcome. Besides, having confronted the ideal and having tested it against the other options, management has a full understanding of the trade-offs as well as the obstacles to implementation.

When it comes time to change the existing distribution system or to scrap it entirely, managers should test modifications on a small scale before committing resources to them. The major problem is that word will spread quickly. The gossip network among dealers and distributors is one of the busiest around.

The process we lay out in this article is not a simple one. Managers are required to focus on something

as insubstantial as quality, or the ideal system, and then to come up with hard numbers to project a reasonable ratio of return to expense. They must even anticipate how adaptable their ideal might be to changes in the law or the political environment. Clearly, there is as much art here as science.

A distribution-system audit may well persuade you to stick with what you've got.

Still, none of the eight steps we outline should be skipped in the interest of apparent expediency. Managerial sophistication will speed the process along, but sophistication alone will be no substitute for going through it. With all the effort reevaluating the system requires, readers may assume that the process always justifies itself by the constructive changes it brings about. In fact, its real value is in the clarity it brings to a critical aspect of doing business.

Recently a specialty grocery products manufacturer discovered that it was getting its products onto supermarket shelves in ways that on the surface looked Rube Goldbergian. It was using an array of third-party players, including food brokers, grocery wholesalers, and health food distributors, some of whom carried out a remarkable range of functions between the manufacturing and the retail level of the distribution chain. When the company drew a structural diagram, it looked like a bowl of spaghetti. Nevertheless, further analysis revealed that the system met all the criteria of an ideal.

The recommendation? "Don't mess with it! Don't touch a thing!" Sometimes the eight-step process explains precisely why you should do nothing to change the distribution system you already have. ▽

Reprint 87411

Ensuring Customer Satisfaction

After the sale is over...

'Relationship management' between buyers and sellers is much like that between husbands and wives

Theodore Levitt

As our economy becomes more service and technology oriented, the dynamics of the sales process will change. The ongoing nature of services and the growing complexity of technology will increasingly necessitate lengthy and involved relationships between buyers and sellers. Thus, the seller's focus will need to shift from simply landing sales to ensuring buyer satisfaction after the purchase. To keep buyers happy, vendors must maintain constructive interaction with purchasers—which includes keeping up on their complaints and future needs. Repeat orders will go to those sellers who have done the best job of nurturing these relationships, the author argues.

Of course, not all products and services require the same degree of relationship cultivating; the longer the period of time over which the service will be extended or the more complex the product being sold, the more attention the seller must give the relationship. Whatever effort is appropriate, though, must be made in a systematic and regular way, which means that sellers must be alert and sensitive. The author offers suggestions for incorporating these qualities into companies' business practices.

Mr. Levitt is the Edward W. Carter Professor of Business Administration and for the past seven years has been head of the marketing area at the Harvard Business School. With this article, he becomes HBR's most frequent contributor—25 articles, beginning with "The Changing Character of Capitalism" (July-August 1956). His most recent articles are "The Globalization of Markets" (May-June 1983) and "Marketing Intangible Products and Product Intangibles" (May-June 1981). His seventh book, The Marketing Imagination, *was published in Fall 1983 by Free Press.*

The relationship between a seller and a buyer seldom ends when a sale is made. Increasingly, the relationship intensifies after the sale and helps determine the buyer's choice the next time around. Such dynamics are found particularly with services and products dealt in a stream of transactions between seller and buyer—financial services, consulting, general contracting, military and space equipment, and capital goods.

The sale, then, merely consummates the courtship, at which point the marriage begins. How good the marriage is depends on how well the seller manages the relationship. The quality of the marriage determines whether there will be continued or expanded business, or troubles and divorce. In some cases divorce is impossible, as when a major construction or installation project is underway. If the marriage that remains is burdened, it tarnishes the seller's reputation.

Companies can avoid such troubles by recognizing at the outset the necessity of managing their relationships with customers. This takes special attention to an often ignored aspect of relationships: time.

The theory of supply and demand presumes that the work of the economic system is time-discrete and bare of human interaction—that an instantaneous, disembodied sales transaction clears the market at the intersection of supply and demand.

Author's note:
This article profited immensely from work done by James L. Crimmins, president of Business Times, Inc., the morning business news show on ESPN Cable, and his colleagues at Playback Associates.

This was never completely accurate and has become less so as product complexity and interdependencies have intensified. Buyers of automated machinery do not, like buyers at a flea market, walk home with their purchases and take their chances. They expect installation services, application aids, parts, postpurchase repair and maintenance, retrofitted enhancements, and vendor R&D to keep the products effective and up to date for as long as possible and to help the company stay competitive.

The buyer of a continuous stream of transactions, like a frozen-food manufacturer that buys its cartons from a packaging company and its cash-management services from a bank, is concerned not only with completing transactions but also with maintaining the process. Due to the growing complexity of military equipment, even the Department of Defense makes most of its purchases in units of less than a hundred and therefore has to repeat transactions often.

Because the purchase cycles of products and major components are increasingly stretched, the needs that must be tended to have changed. Consider the purchase cycles and the changing assurances backing purchases (see *Exhibit I*). Under these conditions, a purchase decision is not a decision to buy an item (to have a casual affair) but a decision to enter a bonded relationship (to get married). This requires of the would-be seller a new orientation and a new strategy.

Selling by itself is no longer enough. Consider the compelling differences between the old and the new selling arrangements *Exhibit II* illustrates. In the selling scheme the seller is located at a distance from buyers and reaches out with a sales department to unload products on them. This is the basis for the notion that a salesperson needs charisma, because it is charisma rather than the product's qualities that makes the sale.

Consider, by contrast, marketing. Here the seller, being physically close to buyers, penetrates their domain to learn about their needs, desires, and fears and then designs and supplies the product with those considerations in mind. Instead of trying to get buyers to want what the seller has, the seller tries to have what they want. The "product" is no longer merely an item but a whole bundle of values that satisfy buyers—an "augmented" product.[1]

Thanks to increasing interdependence, more and more of the world's economic work gets done through long-term relationships between sellers and buyers. It is not a matter of just getting and then holding on to customers. It is more a matter of giving the buyers what they want. Buyers want vendors who keep promises, who'll keep supplying and standing

1 See my article
"Marketing Success Through
Differentiation—Of Anything,"
HBR January-February 1980, p. 83.

Exhibit I   Purchase cycles and assurances

Item	Purchase cycle in years	
Oil field installation	15	to 20
Chemical plant	10	to 15
EDP system	5	to 10
Weapons system	20	to 30
Major components of steel plant	5	to 10
Paper supply contract	5	

Item	Previous assurance	Present assurance
Tankers	Spot	Charter
Apartments	Rental	Cooperative
Auto warranties	10,000 miles	100,000 miles
Technology	Buy	Lease
Labor	Hire	Contracts
Supplies	Shopping	Contracting
Equipment	Repair	Maintenance

Exhibit II   The change from selling to marketing

Selling

Seller → Sales department → Buyer

Marketing

Seller ————————→ Buyer

behind what they promised. The era of the one-night stand is gone. Marriage is both necessary and more convenient. Products are too complicated, repeat negotiations too much of a hassle and too costly. Under these conditions, success in marketing is transformed into the inescapability of a relationship. Interface becomes interdependence.

Under these circumstances, being a good marketer in the conventional sense is not enough. When it takes five years of intensive work between seller and buyer to "deliver" an operating chemical plant or a telecommunications system, much more is required than the kind of marketing that simply lands the contract. The buyer needs assurance at the outset that the two parties can work well together during the long period in which the purchase gets transformed into delivery.

The seller and the buyer have different capital structures, competitive conditions, costs, and incentives driving the commitments they make to each other. The seller has made a sale that is expected to yield a profit. The buyer has bought a tool with which to produce things to yield a profit. For the seller it is the end of the process; for the buyer, only the beginning. Yet their interdependence is inescapable and profound. To make these differently motivated dependencies work, the selling company must understand the relationship and plan its management in advance of the wedding. It can't get out the marriage manual only after trouble has begun.

The product's changing nature

The future will be marked by intense business relationships in all areas of marketing, including frequently purchased consumer goods. Procter & Gamble, copying General Mills's Betty Crocker advisory service, has found that the installation of a consumer hot line to give advice on its products and their uses has cemented customer brand loyalty.

In the industrial setting we have only to review changing perceptions of various aspects of product characteristics to appreciate the new emphasis on relationships (see *Exhibit III*). The common characteristic of the terms in the "future" column of this exhibit is time. What is labeled "item" in the first column was in the past simply a product, something that was bought for its own value. More recently that simple product has not been enough. Instead, buyers have bought augmented products.

During the era we are entering the emphasis will be on systems contracts, and buyer-

seller relationships will be characterized by continuous contact and evolving relationships to effect the systems. The "sale" will be not just a system but a system over time. The value at stake will be the advantages of that total system over time. As the customer gains experience, the technology will decline in importance relative to the system that enables the buyer to realize the benefits of the technology. Services, delivery, reliability, responsiveness, and the quality of the human and organizational interactions between seller and buyer will be more important than the technology itself.

The more complex the system and the more "software" (including operating procedures and protocols, management routines, service components) it requires, the greater the customer's anxieties and expectations. People buy expectations, not things. They buy the expectations of benefits promised by the vendor. When it takes a long time to fulfill the promise (to deliver a new custom-made automated work station, for example) or when fulfillment is continual over a long period (as it is in banking services, fuel deliveries, or shipments of components for assembly operations), the buyer's anxieties build up after the purchase decision is made. Will the delivery be prompt? Will it be smooth and regular? Did we select the best vendor?

Differing expectations

When downstream realities loom larger than up-front promises, what do you do before, during, and after the sale? Who should be responsible for what?

To answer these questions it helps to understand how the promises and behavior of the vendor before the sale is made shape the customer's expectations. It is reasonable for a customer who has been promised the moon to expect it to be delivered. But if those who make the promises are paid commissions before the customer gets everything he bargained for, they're not likely to feel compelled to ensure that the customer gets fully satisfied later. After the sale, they'll rush off to pursue other prey. If marketing plans the sale, sales makes it, manufacturing fulfills it, and service services it, who's in charge and who takes responsibility for the whole process?

Problems arise not only because those who do the selling, the marketing, the manufacturing, and the servicing have varying incentives and views of the customer but also because organizations are one-dimensional. People, with the exception of those who work in sales or marketing, seldom see beyond their company's walls. For those inside those walls, inside is where the work gets done, where the penalties and incentives are doled out, where the budgets and plans

Exhibit III	Perceptions of product values		
Category	**Past**	**Present**	**Future**
Item	Product	Augmented product	System contracts
Sale	Unit	System	System over time
Value	Feature advantages	Technology advantages	System advantages
Leadtime	Short	Long	Lengthy
Service	Modest	Important	Vital
Delivery place	Local	National	Global
Delivery phase	Once	Often	Continually
Strategy	Sales	Marketing	Relationship

Exhibit IV	Varying reactions and perceptions before and during sale process

When the sale is first made

Seller	Buyer
Objective achieved.	Judgment postponed; applies test of time.
Selling stops.	Shopping continues.
Focus goes elsewhere.	Focus on purchase; wants affirmation that expectations have been met.
Tension released.	Tension increased.
Relationship reduced or ended.	Commitment made; relationship intensified.

Throughout the process

Stage of sale		Seller	Buyer
1	Before	Real hope	Vague need
2	Romance	Hot & heavy	Testing & hopeful
3	Sale	Fantasy: bed	Fantasy: board
4	After	Looks elsewhere for next sale	"You don't care"
5	Long after	Indifferent	"Can't this be made better?"
6	Next sale	"How about a new one?"	"Really?"

get made, where engineering and manufacturing are done, where performance is measured, where one's friends and associates gather, where things are managed and manageable. Outside "has nothing to do with me" and is where "you can't change things."

Many disjunctions exist between seller and buyer at various stages of the sales process. These may be simply illustrated, as in *Exhibit IV.*

After the fact

The fact of buying changes the dynamics of the relationship. The buyer expects the seller to remember the purchase as having been a favor bestowed, not as something earned by the seller. Hence it is wrong to assume that getting an account gives you an advantage because you've got a foot in the door. The opposite is more often the case. The buyer that views the sale as a favor conferred on the seller in effect debits the seller's account. The seller owes the buyer one. He is in the position of having to rebuild the relationship from a deficit stance.

In the absence of good management, the relationship deteriorates because both organizations tend naturally to face inward rather than outward toward each other. The natural tendency of relationships, whether in marriage or in business, is toward erosion of sensitivity and attentiveness. Inward orientation by the selling organization leads to insensitivity and unresponsiveness in customer relations. At best the company substitutes bureaucratic formalities for authentic interaction.

A healthy relationship maintains, and preferably expands, the equity and the possibilities that were created during courtship. A healthy relationship requires a conscious and constant fight against the forces of decline. It becomes important for the seller regularly and seriously to consider whether the relationship is improving or deteriorating, whether the promises are being completely fulfilled, whether he is neglecting anything, and how he stands vis-à-vis his competitors. *Exhibit V* compares actions that affect—for better or worse—relationships with buyers.

Building dependencies

One of the surest signs of a bad or declining relationship is the absence of complaints from the customer. Nobody is ever *that* satisfied, especially not over an extended period of time. The customer is either not being candid or not being contacted.

Probably both. The absence of candor reflects the decline of trust and the deterioration of the relationship. Bad things accumulate. Impaired communication is both a symptom and a cause of trouble. Things fester inside. When they finally erupt, it's usually too late or too costly to correct the situation.

We can invest in relationships and we can borrow from them. We all do both, but we seldom account for our actions and almost never manage them. Yet a company's most precious asset is its relationships with its customers. What matters is not whom you know but how you are known to them.

Not all relationships can or need be of the same duration or at the same level of intimacy. These factors depend on the extent of the actual or felt dependency between the buyer and the seller. And of course those dependencies can be extended or contracted through various direct links that can be established between the two parties. Thus, when Bergen Brunswig, the booming drug and health care products distributor, puts computer terminals in its customers' offices to enable them to order directly and get instant feedback regarding their sales and inventory, it creates a new link that helps tie the customer to the vendor.

At the same time, however, the seller can become dependent on the buyer in important ways. Most obvious is vendor reliance on the buyer for a certain percentage of its sales. More subtle is reliance on the buyer for important information, including how the buyer's business will change, how changes will affect future purchases, and what competitors are offering in the way of substitute products or materials, at what prices and including which services. The buyer can also answer questions like these for the vendor: How well is the vendor fulfilling the customer's needs? Is performance up to promises from headquarters? To what new uses is the customer putting the product?

The seller's ability to forecast the buyer's intentions rests on the quality of the overall relationship. In a good relationship the buyer shares plans and expectations with the vendor, or at least makes available relevant information. With that information the vendor can better serve the buyer. Surprises and bad forecasts are symptoms of bad relationships. In such instances, everybody—even the buyer—loses.

Thus, a system of reciprocal dependencies develops. It is up to the seller to nurture the relationship beyond its simple dollar value. In a proper relationship both the buyer and the seller will benefit or the relationship will not last.

Moreover, both parties should understand that the seller's expenses rarely end with acquisition costs. This means that the vendor should work at convincing the customer of the importance of maintaining the vendor's long-term profitability at a comfortable level instead of squeezing to get rock-bottom delivered prices. Unless the costs of the expected post-

Exhibit V   Actions that affect relationships

Positive actions	Negative actions
Initiate positive phone calls	Make only call backs
Make recommendations	Make justifications
Use candid language	Use accommodative language
Use phone	Use correspondence
Show appreciation	Wait for misunderstandings
Make service suggestions	Wait for service requests
Use "we" problem-solving language	Use "owe us" legal language
Get to problems	Respond only to problems
Use jargon or shorthand	Use long-winded communications
Air personality problems	Hide personality problems
Talk of "our future together"	Talk about making good on the past
Routinize responses	Fire drill/emergency responsiveness
Accept responsibility	Shift blame
Plan the future	Rehash the past

Exhibit VI   Cumulative cash flow history of an account

Before product is delivered	After product is delivered

R&D expenses
Presale work
Field and product development

Cash flow +
−

Buyer is expectant

Buyer is happy that progress is made

Buyer encourages vendor spending

Buyer exerts "cash" from vendor in form of "tax" or lower prices unless given reasons early not to

Buyer seeks expanded services with no increase in price

—— Upper level of potential revenue   --- Lower level of potential revenue

••• Actual level of revenue

purchase services are reflected in the price, the buyer will end up paying extra in money, in delays, and in aggravation. The smart relationship manager in the selling company will help the buyer do long-term life-cycle costing to assess the vendor's offering.

Bonds that last

Professional partnerships in law, medicine, architecture, consulting, investment banking, and advertising rate and reward associates by their client relationships. Like any other assets, these relationships can appreciate or depreciate. Their maintenance and enhancement depend not so much on good manners, public relations, tact, charm, window dressing, or manipulation as they do on management. Relationship management requires companywide maintenance, investment, improvement, and even replacement programs. The results can be spectacular.

Examine the case of the North Sea oil and gas fields. Norway and Britain urged and facilitated exploration and development of those resources. They were eager and even generous hosts to the oil companies. The companies, though they spent hundreds of millions of dollars to do the work, didn't fully nurture their relationships. When oil and gas suddenly started to flow, the host countries levied taxes exceeding 90% of the market prices. No one was more surprised than the companies. Why should they have been surprised? Had they built sound relationships with the governments, the politicians, and the voters—by whatever means—so as to have created a sense of mutuality and partnership, they might have moderated the size of the taxes. What would it have been worth?

This is not an isolated occurrence. The same problem crops up in similar circumstances where vendors are required to make heavy expenditures to get accounts and develop products. *Exhibit VI* depicts cash flows to a vendor of this type during the life of the account. During the customer-getting and development period, cash flows are negative and the customer eagerly encourages the expenditures. When the product is delivered or the joint venture becomes operative, cumulative cash flows turn up and finally become positive. In the case of the North Sea, the surprising new high taxes represent the difference between what revenues to the oil companies might have been (the upper level of potential revenue) and what they actually became. With worse relationships they might, of course, have fallen to an even lower level of potential revenue.

Consider also the case of Gillette North America. It has four separate sales forces and special programs for major accounts to ensure Gillette's rapid and smooth response to customers' requirements. Gillette also has a vice president of business relations who has among his major duties cultivation of relationships with major retailers and distributors. He carries out that responsibility via a vast array of ceremonial activities ranging from entertainment at trade association conventions to organization of special events for major accounts in connection with the annual All-Star baseball game, the World Series, the Superbowl, and the NCAA playoffs. These activities establish bonds and affirm reciprocal obligations and benefits.

Some companies now require engineering and manufacturing people to spend time with customers and users in the field—not just to get product and design ideas or feedback regarding present products but also to get to know and to respond to customers in deep and abiding ways so as to build relationships and bonds that last. The Sperry Corporation's much-advertised "listening" campaign has included training employees to listen and communicate effectively with each other and with customers.

All too often company officials take action instead of spending time. It is all too easy to act first and later try to fix the relationship, instead of the other way around. It is all too simple to say, "We'll look into it and call you back" or "Let's get together for lunch sometime." These are tactics of diversion and delay, not of relationship building.

When a purchase cycle is long—as when a beer-making plant contracts with a can-making vendor to build a factory next door or when the U.S. Air Force commits itself to buying a jet engine with a life of 20 to 30 years—the people in the vendor organization who did the selling and those in the customer organization who did the buying will be replaced over the course of those relationships. So, in all likelihood, will the entire upper levels of management on both sides. What must the seller do to ensure continuity of good relations? What is expected of the customer when people who did the buying are changed and gone? Clearly the idea is to build bonds that last no matter who comes and goes.

Making it happen

To effectively manage relationships, managers must meet four requirements:

1   **Awareness.** Understand both the problem and the opportunity areas.

2   **Assessment.** Determine where the company now stands, especially in terms of what's necessary to get the desired results.

3   **Accountability.** Establish regular reporting on individual relationships, and then on group relationships, so that these can be weighed against other measures of performance.

4   **Actions.** Make decisions and allocations and establish routines and communications on the basis of their impact on the targeted relationships. Constantly reinforce awareness and actions.

Relationship management can be institutionalized, but in the process it must also be humanized. One company has regular sensitivity sessions and role-playing seminars in which sales officials assume the buyer role. It also conducts debriefings on meetings with customers. And it requires its customer-contact people (including those who make deliveries and handle receivables) to regularly ask of various accounts the seminal questions: How are we doing in the relationship? Is it going up or down? Are we talking with the right people about the right issues? What have we *not* done lately?

The emphasis on "lately" is not incidental. It reflects the recognition that relationships naturally degrade and have to be reinvigorated. If I owe you a favor, I forget—but you don't. And when I've done you a favor, you feel obligated—but not for long. You ask, "What have you done for me lately?" A relationship credit must be cashed in or it expires, and it must be used soon or it depreciates.

Another way companies can institutionalize relationship management is by establishing routines that ensure the right kinds of customer contacts. A well-known Wall Street investment firm requires its security analysts and salespeople to make regular "constructive" contacts with their institutional customers. *Constructive* is defined as conveying useful information to them. The firm has set up a regular Monday-morning investment strategy "commentary" that analysts and salespeople can convey by telephone to their customers. In addition, each analyst must develop periodic industry commentaries and updates, to be mailed or telephoned to customers. Analysts and salespeople are required to keep logs of these contacts, which are compiled, counted, and communicated to all in a weekly companywide report. Those salespeople and analysts making the fewest contacts have to explain their inaction to supervisors.

The firm allocates end-of-year bonuses on the basis of not only commissions earned from the various institutions but also the number and types of contacts initiated and maintained. Meanwhile, the firm conducts regular sensitivity-training sessions to enhance the contacts and the quality of the relationships. The results, which show that the efforts have been highly successful, are analyzed and made known to all, thus reinforcing the importance of the process.

Relationship management is a special field all its own and is as important to preserving and enhancing the intangible asset commonly known as "goodwill" as is the management of hard assets. The fact that it is probably more difficult makes hard work at it that much more important. ▽

Relationship contracts

Although our relationships change and develop over time, we tend to develop a set of assumptions and expectations in each of them about what our behavior and that of the other "should" be like. Most of these assumptions are not in our awareness, but nonetheless they provide important expectations about how we should "be" in the relationship. It is almost as if an unstated contract develops between us and the other, which we are often not aware of until one of us breaks it. The feelings of surprise or hurt that we sometimes experience over another's behavior when he or she does something or behaves in ways we did not expect is often a signal that some part of an unarticulated contract has been violated. The existence of these contracts does not have to be in our awareness to influence our behavior….

The fact that people do change and develop over time has important implications for developing awareness about relationships that we value and want to last. First is a need for awareness that the other person may be changing in ways that mean that our assumptions about them and about the relationship are out of date. Second, we ourselves may be undergoing changes of which the other person is not aware, so that our present behavior is inconsistent with the other's expectations and creates problems for him or her in the relationship….

…Greater mutual awareness of how each person has changed holds the promise that some conscious accommodation or change might take place that could strengthen or reestablish the relationship. This seems far better than perpetuating a precarious relationship that can only offer the possibility that things could become worse, for reasons that are not understood. The passive acceptance of such a situation can promise only continued anger, frustration, and the anxiety accompanying the realization that what is wrong is either unknown or must be denied. In most cases, efforts to be open will result in making relationships more adaptive, vital, and fulfilling to the people involved, and will allow for the growth of the relationship as well as that of the people in the relationship.

From
Anthony G. Athos and
John J. Gabarro
Interpersonal Behavior
Communication and Understanding in Relationships
(Englewood Cliffs, N.J.: Prentice-Hall, 1978).
© Prentice-Hall.

Reprint 83511

HBR CASE STUDY

Presto Cleaner's new computer system would work great – if it weren't for the customers.

The Case of the Complaining Customer

by Dan Finkelman and Tony Goland

In an effort to improve service, Presto Cleaner installed a new computer system, designed to cut the customers' waiting time and simplify the drop-off and pickup processes. But the system was only a few months old when Mr. J.W. Sewickley, the company president, re-

---

HBR's cases are derived from the experiences of real companies and real people. As written, they are hypothetical, and the names used are fictitious.

---

ceived an angry letter from Mr. George Shelton, whose laundry had been lost by the new system. Mr. Shelton's letter described his experience with Presto Cleaner's complaint-handling operations and demanded compensation and an apology. To respond to the complaint, Mr. Sewickley sent the letter to his customer complaint office, asking for more information. The answer came back from Paul Hoffner. He explained that there were extenuating circumstances and suggested that

some customers may not be worth keeping. Is the customer always right? Where should a company draw the line on compensation and service? What is the best way to handle cases of complaining customers?

Dan Finkelman is a principal in the Cleveland office of McKinsey & Company and leader of the firm's worldwide customer satisfaction and service practice. Tony Goland is a senior engagement manager in the Cleveland office.

10/24/89

Paul,
This letter came
to my attention.
Before I can answer
it, I need your
input. please advise.
JWS

Mr. J.W. Sewickley
President
Presto Cleaner

Dear Mr. Sewickley: October 14, 1989

   My wife and I are angry, frustrated, and disappointed ex-customers. We weren't always that way. In fact, for a year prior to the recent set of events, we were exceptionally pleased with your service. When you opened your store at the intersection of Adams and Broadway, we were delighted. Even though you're not exactly the least expensive dry cleaner in the area, my wife and I felt that the convenience of the location, the extra early and late hours of operation, and the helpfulness of the staff more than made up for the cost.

   That was before you installed your computerized system. The following set of facts will tell you why we are not doing business with Presto Cleaner and what you need to do to get us back as satisfied customers.

   July 28: I dropped off some laundry at the store, and the counterperson introduced me to the new computer system. I filled out a "preference card" (light starch for my shirts, folded in a box, and so on) that was entered into the computer. I selected an identification code number (my phone number) and bought a special bag customized with my identification number. The bag was only $3, no big deal. Ideally, the next time I had laundry, all I would have to do was put my laundry in the bag and drop it off. No waiting in line, no waiting for a receipt, the computer knew what I wanted done. When it came time to pick it up, I would just pay, get the laundry, and go. Easy, convenient, time saving. *Supposedly.*

   August 4: My wife stopped in to pick up the July 28 order and dropped off the bag with the new laundry (4 of my shirts, 2 blouses, 1 suit, 1 skirt). The counterperson had her fill out her own preference card and entered that information into the computer.

   August 10: On the way home from work, I stopped in to make a drop-off and a pickup. Guess what, Mr. Sewickley? I needed to buy a second special bag if I wanted to use the new system every time. I had to stand in line and wait my turn and finally give my order to the person behind the counter. It took forever. The great new system required the counterperson to enter every item, its color or other distinguishing feature, and also what operation I wanted done (clean, press, and so on). It took more than ten minutes. The old system was actually faster.

   Then when I finished with the drop-off, I told the counterperson I also had an order to pick up. She asked me for the receipt. I explained that I had used the new computerized system with the bags, so I didn't have a receipt. She asked for my identification number. When she punched it into the computer, it said that my wife had picked up the order earlier in the day.

   When I got home, I asked my wife if she had picked up the order. She said she had because she had a business meeting the next day and needed a suit that was at the cleaners. I asked about the bag, and after looking everywhere, including the backseat of the car, we finally determined that she had picked up a previous order and definitely not the order with the special bag. Missing were 4 shirts, 2 blouses, 1 suit, and 1 skirt.

   August 11: I called the store from work and explained the problem. The counterperson was very courteous, apologized, and said that the store would be searched for the missing items.

   August 14: I went to the store to pick up the last order. I stood in line, waiting for roughly 15 minutes for the two people in front of me to struggle through the computer system. I finally got my order and asked about the lost clothing. After a lot of asking around, the counterperson finally determined that the clothes had not turned up at the store. We next tried to locate the order in the computer, only to discover that when my wife and I had chosen identification numbers, she had used our home phone number and I had used my business number. After searching the computer using both numbers, we still turned up nothing. The counterperson said he would put a tracer on the order back at the plant.

   August 15: My wife left work early to take our next laundry order to one of your competitors that has a store near our house. It's open only until 5:30, but there's less nonsense.

   August 19: I picked up the order from the nearby Kwik N' Klean on my way to my favorite men's store to buy four new shirts. I didn't have enough shirts to make it through two weeks of work because of the four that were still missing. I am enclosing the sales slip for the four new shirts. I fully expect you to reimburse me for these shirts.

   August 22: I called the store to see if my clothes had been found. There was still no word from the plant.

   August 25: I called the store again. It had heard from the plant, and the plant did not have the clothing.

   Why, Mr. Sewickley, did they not call me? I asked how to pursue a claim for lost items and learned that I should call a Mr. Paul Hoffner at the office.

I immediately called Mr. Hoffner and was told that he was not available. I left a message for him to call back as soon as possible.

August 26: I called back again. Mr. Hoffner was not available. I left the same message.

August 27: I called back again. Mr. Hoffner was not available. I asked if there was anyone else who could handle a claim for lost items and was told that only Mr. Hoffner could do that.

August 31: Mr. Hoffner called. I told him that I wanted to put in a claim. He was totally unaware of the situation, so I had to explain it to him. He suggested that he call the store and the plant to find out if there was any progress. I got the distinct impression that he didn't believe me and that he felt he needed to check with the store to make sure that I really was a customer and that there really was missing laundry. I assured Mr. Hoffner that I was a real customer. In fact, for more than a year, my wife and I have averaged between $20 and $30 worth of dry cleaning every week. Despite my assurances, Mr. Hoffner insisted that he had to check before anything could happen. When I pushed to find out what the process was, Mr. Hoffner said that if the clothing really was lost, I could fill out a claim form and apply for compensation.

September 7: A week had passed with no word from Mr. Hoffner. I called. He wasn't available. I left a message.

September 11: Still no word from Mr. Hoffner. I called and miracle of miracles, he answered the phone. After all that time, the only thing he could tell me was that neither the store nor the plant could find the clothes. I asked him to send the claim form.

September 18: No claim form had yet arrived in the mail, so I called Mr. Hoffner again. I got him and asked about the form. He said he had delayed sending it because he was sure that the clothes would be found. I insisted that he send the form immediately.

September 21: The claim form arrived, and I discovered that it required that I attach both the original purchase receipt for the clothes and the counter receipt for the laundry order. Mr. Sewickley, do you keep your year-old receipts for clothing? And with the new computer system, there are no counter receipts!

It took two more calls to get through to Mr. Hoffner to complain about these requirements. He said that they were necessary to guard the company against fraud. He did acknowledge that since your own system no longer produced counter receipts, I couldn't be expected to send them in. But as far as the receipts for the clothes were concerned, he suggested that I go back through our charge card records to come up with the proof of purchase. I flatly refused. I told Mr. Hoffner that we have done more than $1,000 worth of business with Presto Cleaner over the past year and that we were not in the business of extorting money from dry cleaners. Further, I told him that if my word wasn't good enough for him, he could kiss our business good-bye, along with that of our friends and colleagues at work, who would soon hear all about the Presto Cleaner way of doing business.

September 22: Having had a terribly busy week, we forgot that my wife needed a dress cleaned for a business function Saturday night. Since it was Friday morning when we discovered this, our only real option was for my wife to drop off the dress at Presto Cleaner in the morning.

September 23: I went in to pick up the dress. The woman behind the counter recognized me and told me that the store had found our lost clothes. Apparently, they had been mysteriously included in another customer's order and only just now returned. She had no clue how this could have happened with the new system. She was, as usual, cheerful, apologetic, and polite about the mix-up. I paid for the order, picked up the dress, and went home.

September 25: Since there was no way to call your office over the weekend, I waited until Monday to try to reach Mr. Hoffner. He was again unavailable, so I left him the last message he will ever get from me: the clothes were found, but I would still like to talk to him.

Mr. Sewickley, that was more than two weeks ago, and I still haven't heard from Mr. Hoffner. I am outraged by this entire episode, by the way your company treats customers, by Mr. Hoffner's conduct, by the lack of communication, and by the ridiculous system you introduced. I am particularly incensed at having to pay for clothes that were delivered almost two months late and by having to purchase new clothes to cover your company's mistake.

I expect the following: a full refund for the order that was lost; full payment for the four shirts that I had to buy to make up for the lost order; and a full apology from Mr. Hoffner. If all of those are forthcoming, I might consider giving your company another chance at my business. Otherwise, my wife and I will never patronize your company again.

Sincerely,

George Shelton

George Shelton

Memo
To: JWS
From: Paul Hoffner   *P. H.*   Oct. 29, 1989
Re: Customer Complaint

This is in response to your memo requesting background information to respond to the customer complaint of Mr. George Shelton. I have reviewed his letter as well as our own file concerning this matter. I am convinced that we did make a good-faith effort to do right by Mr. Shelton, although he may not recognize it as such. Nevertheless, should you wish to mollify the customer, I would be perfectly happy to play the role of fall guy if it would help. As far as extending compensation to the customer is concerned, his demands seem to me far in excess of any real liability: he did get his clothes back, he will keep the four new shirts and use them, as well. I would certainly extend an apology to him—if he would like it from me, fine; I assume that it would be even more satisfactory coming from you, along with an offer to clean his next order free of charge.

Having said this, there are some mitigating circumstances that you should be aware of. I would not share these with the customer, but present them to you so that you will understand more accurately and fully what really happened, rather than what this one customer says happened. Again, that does not mean that a mistake was not made; there was a mistake, and we should take responsibility for that. But we acted in a way consistent with company policy and operations. Let me describe what really happened:

1.) The customer dropped off his clothing on literally the first day of operation of the new computerized system—a system that everyone at headquarters agrees is the key to our future success. Everyone also agrees that there will be problems, including, unfortunately, some lost customers. Mr. Shelton may be one such example. As you remember, because of delays with the system vendor and the software, we had only one week to train our people on the new system. Also, as I'm sure you're aware, not all of our store personnel are great at using this technology. It has taken more time than expected to get them to understand all of the steps they have to take to prevent mistakes.

2.) As I suspected all along, the real problem in this case was that the clothing was picked up by another customer. This is not that unusual. When it happens, we must rely on the goodwill of our customers to return what is not theirs. This time, because the customer was an infrequent user of our service, it took him more than four weeks to bring the clothes back in. Also, he dropped the clothes off at a different store. Unfortunately, we have more than one case of lost clothes at a time (please note all the letters of complaint that you *don't* have, proof that the system works most of the time), so we cannot call every customer and ask him or her to come in and identify the clothes. Our policy, therefore, is simply to wait for customers to come in and then offer them a chance to identify the clothes.

3.) Much of Mr. Shelton's gripe concerns the early period (approximately August 12 through August 25) during which time he felt he was kept in the dark. But as you know, our process is designed to get the stores and the plant to figure out problems. My written record shows that the plant did two thorough searches before reporting the lack of results to the store. It's hard to fault it for thoroughness. Apparently, the store also delayed referring the customer to me, probably thinking that the clothes would turn up and, perhaps, not wishing to have to report bad news concerning our new computer system. The process also may have taken this much time because of our standing company policy that requires all reports between stores, the plant, and the office to be in writing.

4.) After I spoke with the customer, I spent the next ten days or so checking with the store and the plant in an attempt to determine what exactly had happened and to locate and identify the clothes. By the end of the first week, I felt sure that the clothes had mistakenly gone to another customer. But there was no way to retrieve them, other than to wait for them to turn up. I did not tell the customer this, of course; after years of experience, I have found that customers only get more upset at the idea that a stranger has their clothes.

5.) Unbeknownst to me, the missing clothes were returned to the Adams and Broadway location on September 14. The customer who had mistakenly received the clothes dropped them off at one of our suburban locations, which then forwarded them to the plant. The plant used our standard identification process, sent them to the Adams and Broadway store, and then wrote me a memo, which I received on September 23. Before I could call the customer and inform him, he had picked up his clothes. I did get one more very angry message from the customer, which I decided not to return, since further communication would unlikely be of any benefit.

6.) Mr. Shelton's letter has several misstatements of fact. While there is no point in disputing these points with him, you should know the following:

(a) I did not delay in sending him a claim form. I sent the form after he requested it and do not know why it was not received. When he called back on September 18, I sent another form. I did not tell him that I had delayed in sending the form. I told him we were trying to locate and identify his clothes.

(b) When I spoke to the customer regarding the standard claim form, I did not tell him to produce proof of purchase. I told him it would be helpful to us if he could get a good estimate of the value of the items.

7.) As you can tell from the tone of Mr. Shelton's letter, he is a very demanding, persistent individual. What his letter does not tell you, however, is that he inundated us with the sheer volume of his calls. Given the number and frequency of his calls, there was no way for me to demonstrate progress on his problem before he called again. When he writes that he "left a message," you should know that his "messages" were usually cryptic. He often did not leave a phone number and, on more than one occasion, even refused to leave his name. For example, he would say, "You know who this is." My secretary found all of this quite distressing. Moreover, I've never run into a customer so anxious to be compensated.

This brings up several interesting questions: How do we make up for the mistake we made without being browbeaten into excess compensation? For example, his four shirts would cost us more than $200; refunding his order would add another $35; if I had swiftly processed his original claim, it would have come to over $600.

In other words, despite Mr. Shelton's threats, I think our system worked. Although we did misplace his clothes, he got everything back, and we avoided a major expense. Now some restitution, such as one free order and a written apology, should be enough. If that is not good enough for Mr. Shelton, it seems to me we should ask, "Aren't there some customers we are better off losing?" Maybe this is a customer that Kwik N' Klean deserves!

How can Presto Cleaner keep Mr. Shelton as a customer? Should it try?

Four authorities on customer service consider Presto Cleaner's customer complaint.

Presto Cleaner's behavior could cost it $500,000 a year.

Mr. Sewickley should replace Paul Hoffner. His response – and consequently Presto Cleaner's – to the situation appears to be oriented toward driving customers away, not toward building a business.

First, look at the situation. Presto Cleaner should be commended for implementing computer-based systems that increase the speed of service and eliminate paper pushing. However, the decision to introduce the system with limited employee training and no advance customer preparation or education created a nightmare. This could have been avoided. Each operating unit could have invested resources to set up a separate line or section of the store to indoctrinate customers in the new system without disrupting the normal flow of business. Hoffner resorts to identifying the rushed implementation of the system as an acceptable excuse for the customer problem. This clearly is not the case.

Certainly, mistakes will happen – all organizations make them. But mistakes provide organizations like Presto Cleaner the opportunity to

LEONARD A. SCHLESINGER *is associate professor of business administration at the Harvard Business School.*

recover in ways that actually build customer loyalty rather than lose business. This fact seems to escape Paul Hoffner. He appears to have adopted an internally focused and strictly rational approach to search for the missing clothing. He therefore ignores the customer's emotions. Unreturned phone calls and unsent forms serve only to turn a small mistake into a big one. The assumption that Presto Cleaner must actively guard against the potential of customers' fraudulent claims pervades all aspects of his relationship with Mr. Shelton. It is an attitude that other customers and the Presto Cleaner staff must notice as well. If you regard your customers as a band of potential cheats and believe that you must protect yourself from them, how can you possibly deliver to them the kind of service they deserve?

Having blown several opportunities to impress Mr. Shelton with Presto Cleaner's desire to solve his problem, Mr. Sewickley now faces the question of restitution for the situation. Mr. Shelton is clearly angry, and his request is undoubtedly greater than it would have been a few weeks earlier had Presto Cleaner handled the situation more ably. Paul Hoffner believes the request is absurd and actively encourages Mr. Sewickley to consider losing the Sheltons as customers. But we know from consumer research that for every complaint such as Mr. Shelton's, there are 20 or more customers who leave quietly and unnoticed and thereby provide the organization with no opportunity to learn from its mistakes. Mr. Hoffner is about to ensure that no learning occurs even when the customer complains. Purely in economic terms, the loss could be enormous. Assume that Presto Cleaner manages to lose one customer a day (not an unreasonable assumption given the company's behavior in this situation). Based on Mr. Shelton's estimates of his laundry expenditures, the annual revenue loss from such an unnoticed customer defection would reach almost $500,000.

In that context, Mr. Shelton's request is not at all unreasonable. If I were Mr. Sewickley, I would use the opportunity presented by the complaint letter to make one last attempt at service recovery. I would immediately reimburse Mr. Shelton's $235. But rather than write a simple apology letter, I would deliver the check myself and stress the following points:

☐ What happened was unacceptable; there are no excuses for it.

☐ Presto Cleaner will reimburse all out-of-pocket losses.

☐ Presto Cleaner does not want to lose Mr. Shelton and will do *whatever* it takes to get him back.

My assumption is that this dramatic gesture will bring Mr. Shelton back to Presto Cleaner.

Lastly, Mr. Sewickley should use this complaint and the company's response as a learning opportunity for the company. The organization must establish a clear model of customer relations and service standards at the top. The Shelton complaint provides an opportunity for a broad discussion of customer problem resolution. In a competitive business environment, the risks of not capitalizing on this opportunity could be catastrophic.

should act on the principle that, having made service mistakes, Presto Cleaner should bear all the customer's out-of-pocket costs. In addition, to demonstrate that anything short of highly satisfying service is not Presto Cleaner's way, Sewickley should enclose the $50 certificate.

This solution is based on the four-rung customer satisfaction ladder we're working to implement at Citibank. The system works like this: rung 1, customers say "This company doesn't work"; rung 2, customers' basic service requirements are met; rung 3, customers get service personalized to their needs; and rung 4, customers say, "The service wows me!"

Ironically, Presto Cleaner's new computer system was geared to take the company's second rung, basically satisfying service, to a higher level of personalized service—rung 3. However, the total service failure moved Shelton down to rung 1. Therefore, a rung 4, "Presto Cleaner wows me!" action is called for. Sewickley's restorative actions most likely will regain Shelton's business. It should also enhance Presto Cleaner's reputation in the long term.

The larger issue on Sewickley's agenda must be to modernize Presto Cleaner's quality performance, just as he's working to update his technology. Both service and infrastructure should be state-of-the-art. Shelton's experience suggests there is much to do. For example, Presto Cleaner's policies to deal with customer problems require a thorough review. How can the stores and plant respond more quickly to customer difficulties? How can quality be designed into new procedures *before* they're introduced? Such policy reviews, interdepartmental teamwork, and quality-assurance issues are classical service-quality priorities. Sewickley should establish and communicate profitability-based customer satisfaction as a primary company goal and implement a diversified service-quality program.

Two imperatives are key to Presto Cleaner.

Strive for problem-free service. Presto Cleaner needs to "do it right the first time." As Shelton's experience illustrates, customer prob-

Every business should aim to close its customer complaint department.

Presto Cleaner has a dual challenge: to regain Mr. Shelton's business and ensure consistent customer-satisfying service to all customers. Both issues underscore why this is really "A Case *for* Problem-Free Service." While responsive service after the sale is a prerequisite for organizations today, their primary goal should be

DINAH NEMEROFF *is corporate director of customer affairs at Citicorp/Citibank.*

problem-free service. Every business should aim to close its customer complaint department! Problem prevention, not problem resolution, is a superordinate service-quality objective.

Unfortunately, Shelton already is knee-deep in problems, and these have grown geometrically, as is often the case. Presto Cleaner's Mr. Hoffner, his interactions with Shelton, and his lack of follow-through have made a bad situation worse. To remedy the situation, Presto Cleaner's president, Mr. Sewickley, should take some immediate first steps. First, he should send a letter of apology to Shelton with two enclosures: a $235 check, to cover the $35 charge for the delayed order and the $200 cost of four new shirts, and a $50 certificate for future Presto Cleaner service. He lems are costly to resolve, lead directly to lost business, and erode customer goodwill.

Even with first-rate customer service, customers do not "fully recover" from service problems. Citibank research shows that customers who've had problems resolved *to their satisfaction* are, nevertheless, on average 20% less satisfied than problem-free customers. Also, Presto Cleaner's management should not make the common mistake of viewing customer complaints as a comprehensive report card of the company's service. Complaints are a small subset of customer problems, registered by the vocal few; the majority of troubled customers silently desert to competitors. Presto Cleaner executives should understand the type, frequency, and severity of customer problems to implement a problem-free service plan. Such experiences must be seen from the customer's perspective. In large-scale organizations – or when employees rarely interact with customers – systematic customer feedback must be used to gather this crucial data.

Improve customer service. Because it's a rare business that can close its customer complaint department, this service function must be efficient and responsive.

Presto Cleaner's customer service problems begin with the customer-unfriendly computer system and Paul Hoffner, but they do not end there. A Presto Cleaner customer with a problem is in a limbo of missing laundry, knowing neither what to expect nor how to get help.

I recommend three strategies we've found valuable at Citibank:
☐ Trust the customer. Service policies that assume customers are honest, and it's only the occasional crook who must be caught, are the appropriate ethical standard.
☐ First-request service. A customer should only have to contact a business once to have his or her problem solved or question answered – ideally, this can be done immediately. If this isn't possible, the business takes on the follow-up burden.
☐ Manage customers' expectations. When follow-up is necessary, tell-

ing the customer what to expect can significantly increase his or her satisfaction. When the service investigations department in one Citibank business instituted this particular procedure, specifying time frames for next steps, customers' satisfaction increased by 40%.

Such service improvements are neither easily nor quickly made, in Presto Cleaner or any organization. In fact, they can be expensive to

Mr. Sewickley should "buy the problem."

There are three rules of thumb for creating an effective customer service focus in an organization: understand and respond to customers' expectations, do whatever it takes to be perceived as "easy to do business with," and be good at problem solving. Presto Cleaner has done an excellent job of ignoring all three.

In our studies, good recovery – fixing things that have gone wrong for the customer – accounts for 38.7% of the differences between companies perceived as very good or very bad at serving customers. This has proven to be an especially important distinguisher in retail operations like Presto Cleaner.

For the long term, Mr. Sewickley is going to have to do four things to ensure that the level of problem solving at Presto Cleaner is at least competitive. First, he'll have to make it clear that customer-contact employees, like Paul Hoffner, are expected to go

implement, since up-front investment is frequently required. Nevertheless, the long-term payback is rewarding. A business *can* significantly decrease its cost of quality – foremost by preventing problems, not just fixing them. And when a company consistently provides customer-satisfying service, that business can keep and grow its customer base and earn more of each customer's business.

RON ZEMKE *is president of Performance Research Associates in Minneapolis, Minnesota and author of* The Service Edge *(New American Library, 1988).*

out of their way to solve customer problems. Second, he'll have to set standards for both response time and appropriateness of redress. Third, he must see that customer-contact people are henceforth trained to deal with customers who have been, or believe that they have been, wronged by the company. And finally, he is going to have to scrap his marvelous new system or get help redesigning it from a customer-use point of view. As it stands, the new system threatens to make Presto Cleaner about as customer friendly as a state department of motor vehicles.

Right now, however, Mr. Sewickley must take over as Presto Cleaner's chief problem solver. It is especially important that he not follow Mr. Hoffner's advice and write off the Sheltons. Through word-of-mouth, the Sheltons can do a great deal of damage to the business. A simple "You won't believe how the dry cleaner messed us around!" tale, told often enough, can cost Presto Cleaner as much as 2% of annual revenues. Beyond that, Hoffner's assumption that the Sheltons are a lost cause is probably incorrect. The fact that they bothered to write to the company – something less than 10% of unhappy customers will do – suggests that they want to be coaxed back into the Presto Cleaner fold.

Here's what Mr. Sewickley should do to make it easy for the Sheltons to continue being Presto Cleaner customers. Call George Shelton and apologize – profusely, if necessary. The goal is to make sure that the customer knows that Sewickley doesn't condone lackadaisical treatment of customers or consider problems such as the one the Sheltons experienced as par for the course. And he should be prepared to listen more than he talks. Mr. Shelton probably has a large amount of pent-up frustration that he wants to dump on someone. So let him dump it. It won't cost a dime to hear him out, and frequently the sum and substance of what an upset customer wants is to be heard. Sewickley should try to enlist Mr. Shelton both in solving the problem his family encountered and in suggesting ways that the new system can be made more user friendly. Until now, Shelton has been denied any sense of control over the situation. Give him back some control. Enlisting upset customers to create acceptable solutions also works to bring them from an upset and irrational mind-set to a thinking and reasonable one.

If necessary, Mr. Sewickley should be prepared to "buy the problem" – spend the $235, the cost of the new

shirts and the dry cleaning order. The odds are, however, that Mr. Shelton will drop his demands that Presto Cleaner pay for his replacement shirts once he is talking to the president.

Remember: Sewickley is trying to install a new system. If too many customers are walking around saying bad things about the new way of doing business with Presto Cleaner, there will be no business to do.

And he should follow up with some form of symbolic atonement. He definitely has to send a personalized follow-up letter that refers to their conversation and what will happen as a result of it. But at this point, an additional gesture is necessary. A certificate for free work is OK, flowers would be better.

In the last analysis, Mr. Sewickley is both arbiter and role model for customer relations and customer treatment at Presto Cleaner. If he "blows off" a customer who is initially unreasonable or uses bad language or is simply unpleasant, Mr. Hoffner and every counter clerk in every store will do the same. If Mr. Sewickley shows patience and understanding and evidences a sincere desire to do what it takes to keep Presto Cleaner customers happy and coming back, everyone in his employ will follow suit.

should say thank you. This company should train its employees to listen to customers and change fundamental attitudes so that customers' complaints are viewed as opportunities for positive change, not as reasons to be defensive.

Quality management involves changing attitudes at every level of the company. It is not just for managers. Nor is it just a question of implementing technology and systems. The problem in this instance lies not in the details of what happened but in the flawed values embedded in the procedure.

Mr. Shelton's disappointment stems from bad customer service rather than bad technology. Customer dissatisfaction is often based on emotions, but when asked to explain why they are dissatisfied, customers give rational explanations – even when they are not the real cause. Let me illustrate. When I worked with SAS years ago to improve the company's service, we asked flight attendants to distribute forms asking customers to rate the service. I observed that the process itself was flawed: attendants did not make eye contact, and when customers asked, the attendants would not explain the reason for the forms.

Not surprisingly, customers responded negatively. And when they did, they commented on what I call hard service quality: material aspects such as the space between the seats, waiting time, punctuality of flights, even the fact that champagne was served in plastic glasses.

I then trained attendants to interact better with customers – letting them know why the forms were being distributed or why planes were not on time. After that, the customers responded to the forms by saying they were satisfied. And they named all the same hard qualities as the reasons for their satisfaction! When people are not aware of the "soft" qualities for their dissatisfaction, they invent a lot of socially "reasonable" explanations as justification.

Likewise, the problem here is not the specific incidents that took place but the attitude Mr. Shelton encountered. Had Mr. Hoffner demonstrated a genuine interest in

Send Shelton to dinner and Hoffner to the front lines.

Presto Cleaner's poor service on the front lines reflects the unresponsive and irresponsible employee atti-

CLAUS MØLLER is president of Time Management International, a management development company in Denmark.

tudes of upper and middle management. Mr. Hoffner is not the villain in this case but the victim of a service-management culture that has not built a support system that encourages employees to demonstrate a positive attitude toward the customer.

Customers who take the time and energy to complain are doing companies a favor. They help companies stay in business. Mr. Hoffner must change his attitude; Presto Cleaner should too. When customers complain to Presto Cleaner, employees

Mr. Shelton's problem and given less attention to defending himself, I doubt that the customer would have been dissatisfied. Instead of showing interest in Mr. Shelton's problems, Mr. Hoffner refused to admit to either his customer or his boss that he might be wrong. He is more interested in making the customer wrong than in admitting his own error. He treats the customer as an irritant.

The actions of Mr. Hoffner signal a deeper flaw in the company—which clearly has no defined service policy. Companies should design systems so that employees relate to customers—not technology. Presto Cleaner has flip-flopped its priorities by implementing a computer system that seems to have been designed more for the shop and company than the clients! At least that is the signal sent to its customers. Presto Cleaner also needs to use its time better. If this company spent the same amount of money and time on motivating its staff that it does on writing notes and memos, it would be much better off.

Clearly the company must improve the attitudes of its staff by creating an environment that promotes the best in people. I distinguish between "internal service"—how employees are treated within a company—and "external service"—how employees treat customers. The external service-quality will never exceed internal service-quality. Companies must create responsive attitudes through internal service. Companies must give employees responsibility to make decisions and be prepared for them to make mistakes. They must treat employees as they expect employees to treat customers. One goal to motivate people is to suggest that they treat their customers as they would treat guests in their homes.

I recommend that the company give Mr. Shelton what he requests—along with something extra, such as a complimentary dinner for him and his wife. I also suggest that Mr. Hoffner work on the front line for a while to see how the new system is working and to stay in touch with customers. ▽

Reprint 90304

No-quibble guarantees are self-fulfilling—
they promise quality and produce it.

The Power of Unconditional Service Guarantees

by CHRISTOPHER W.L. HART

When you buy a car, a camera, or a toaster oven, you receive a warranty, a guarantee that the product will work. How often do you receive a warranty for auto repair, wedding photography, or a catered dinner? Virtually never. Yet it is here, in buying services, that the assurance of a guarantee would presumably count most.

Many business executives believe that, by definition, services simply can't be guaranteed. Services are generally delivered by human beings, who are known to be less predictable than machines, and they are usually produced at the same time they are consumed. It is one thing to guarantee a camera, which

Al Burger *started* with an unconditional guarantee and built his company around it.

can be inspected before a customer sets eyes on it and which can be returned to the factory for repairs. But how can you preinspect a car tune-up or send an unsuccessful legal argument or bad haircut back for repair? Obviously you can't.

But that doesn't mean customer satisfaction can't be guaranteed. Consider the guarantee offered by

"Bugs" Burger Bug Killers (BBBK), a Miami-based pest-extermination company that is owned by S.C. Johnson & Son.

Most of BBBK's competitors claim that they will reduce pests to "acceptable levels"; BBBK promises to eliminate them entirely. Its service guarantee to hotel and restaurant clients promises:

■ You don't owe one penny until all pests on your premises have been eradicated.

■ If you are ever dissatisfied with BBBK's service, you will receive a refund for up to 12 months of the company's services—plus fees for another exterminator of your choice for the next year.

■ If a guest spots a pest on your premises, BBBK will pay for the guest's meal or room, send a letter of apology, and pay for a future meal or stay.

■ If your facility is closed down due to the presence of roaches or rodents, BBBK will pay any fines, as well as all lost profits, *plus* $5,000.

In short, BBBK says, "If we don't satisfy you 100%, we don't take your money."

Christopher W.L. Hart is an assistant professor at the Harvard Business School, where he teaches a course on service management. As a researcher and consultant, he helps companies design and implement service-guarantee and quality-improvement programs.

How successful is this guarantee? The company, which operates throughout the United States, charges up to ten times more than its competitors and yet has a disproportionately high market share in its operating areas. Its service quality is so outstanding that the company rarely needs to make good on its guarantee (in 1986 it paid out only $120,000 on sales of $33 million—just enough to prove that its promises aren't empty ones).

A main reason that the "Bugs" Burger guarantee is a strong model for the service industry is that its founder, Al Burger, began with the concept of the unconditional guarantee and worked backward, designing his entire organization to support the no-pests guarantee—in short, he started with a vision of error-free service. In this article, I will explain why the service guarantee can help your organization institutionalize superlative performance.

What a Good Service Guarantee Is

Would you be willing to offer a guarantee of 100% customer satisfaction—to pay your dissatisfied customer to use a competitor's service, for example? Or do you believe that promising error-free service is a crazy idea?

Not only is it not crazy, but *committing* to error-free service can help force a company to *provide* it. It's a little like skiing. You've got to lean over your skis as you go down the hill, as if willing yourself to fall. But if you edge properly, you don't fall or plunge wildly; you gain control while you pick up speed.

Similarly, a strong service guarantee that puts the customer first doesn't necessarily lead to chaos and failure. If designed and implemented properly, it enables you to get control over your organization—with clear goals and an information network that gives you the data you need to improve performance. BBBK and other service companies show that a service guarantee is not only possible—it's a boon to performance and profits and can be a vehicle to market dominance.

Most existing service guarantees don't really do the job: they are limited in scope and difficult to use. Lufthansa guarantees that its customers will make their connecting flights *if* there are no delays due to weather or air-traffic control problems. Yet these two factors cause fully 95% of all flight delays. Bank of America will refund up to six months of checking-account fees if a customer is dissatisfied with any aspect of its checking-account service. However, the customer must close the account to collect the modest $5 or $6 per month fee. This guarantee won't win

any prizes for fostering repeat business—a primary objective of a good guarantee.

A service guarantee loses power in direct proportion to the number of conditions it contains. How effective is a restaurant's guarantee of prompt service *except* when it's busy? A housing inspector's guarantee to identify all potential problems in a house *except for* those not readily apparent? Squaw Valley in California guarantees "your money back" to any skier who has to wait more than ten minutes in a lift line. But it's not that easy: the skier must first pay $1 and register at the lodge as a beginner, intermediate, or expert; the guarantee is operative only if *all* lifts at the skier's skill level exceed the ten minutes in any half-hour period; and skiers must check with a "ski hostess" at the end of the day to "win" a refund. A Squaw Valley spokesperson said the resort had made just one payout under the guarantee in a year and a half. No wonder!

What is a good service guarantee? It is (1) unconditional, (2) easy to understand and communicate, (3) meaningful, (4) easy (and painless) to invoke, and (5) easy and quick to collect on.

Unconditional. The best service guarantee promises customer satisfaction unconditionally, without exceptions. Like that of L.L. Bean, the Freeport, Maine retail store and mail-order house: "100% satisfaction in every way...." An L.L. Bean customer can return a product at any time and get, at his or her option, a replacement, a refund, or a credit. Reputedly, if a customer returns a pair of L.L. Bean boots after ten years, the company will replace them with new boots and no questions. Talk about customer assurance!

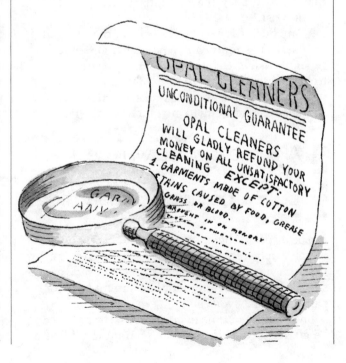

DRAWINGS BY PAUL MEISEL

Customers shouldn't need a lawyer to explain the "ifs, ands, and buts" of a guarantee – because ideally there shouldn't be any conditions; a customer is either satisfied or not.

If a company cannot guarantee all elements of its service unconditionally, it should unconditionally guarantee the elements that it can control. Lufthansa cannot promise on-time arrival, for example, but it could guarantee that passengers will be satisfied with its airport waiting areas, its service on the ground and in the air, and its food quality – or simply guarantee overall satisfaction.

Easy to Understand and Communicate. A guarantee should be written in simple, concise language that pinpoints the promise. Customers then know precisely what they can expect and employees know precisely what's expected of them. "Five-minute" lunch service, rather than "prompt" service, creates clear expectations, as does "no pests," rather than "pest control."

Meaningful. A good service guarantee is meaningful in two respects. First, it guarantees those aspects of your service that are important to your customers. It may be speedy delivery. Bennigan's, a restaurant chain, promises 15-minute service (or you get a free meal) at lunch, when many customers are in a hurry to get back to the office, but not at dinner, when fast service is not considered a priority to most patrons.

In other cases, price may be the most important element, especially with relatively undifferentiated commodities like rental cars or commercial air travel. By promising the lowest prices in town, stereo shops assuage customers' fears that if they don't go to every outlet in the area they'll pay more than they ought to.

L.L. Bean will replace its boots – even after ten years' use.

Second, a good guarantee is meaningful financially; it calls for a significant payout when the promise is not kept. What should it be – a full refund? An offer of free service the next time? A trip to Monte Carlo? The answer depends on factors like the cost of the service, the seriousness of the failure, and customers' perception of what's fair. A money-back payout should be large enough to give customers an incentive to invoke the guarantee if dissatisfied. The adage "Let the punishment fit the crime" is an appropriate guide. At one point, Domino's Pizza (which is based in Ann Arbor, Michigan but operates worldwide) promised "delivery within 30 minutes or the

pizza is free." Management found that customers considered this too generous; they felt uncomfortable accepting a free pizza for a mere 5- or 15-minute delay and didn't always take advantage of the guarantee. Consequently, Domino's adjusted its guarantee to "delivery within 30 minutes or $3 off," and customers appear to consider this commitment reasonable.

Easy to Invoke. A customer who is already dissatisfied should not have to jump through hoops to invoke a guarantee; the dissatisfaction is only exacerbated when the customer has to talk to three different people, fill out five forms, go to a different location, make two telephone calls, send in written proof of purchase with a full description of the events, wait for a written reply, go somewhere else to see someone to verify all the preceding facts, and so on.

Traveler's Advantage – a division of CUC International – has, in principle, a great idea: to guarantee the lowest price on the accommodations it books. But to invoke the guarantee, customers must prove the lower competing price by booking with another agency. That's unpleasant work. Cititravel, a subsidiary of Citicorp, has a better approach. A customer who knows of a lower price can call a toll-free number and speak with an agent, as I did recently. The agent told me that if I didn't have proof of the lower fare, she'd check competing airfares on her computer screen. If the lower fare was there, I'd get that price. If not, she would call the competing airline. If the price was confirmed, she said, "We'll refund your money so fast, you won't believe it – because we want you to be our customer." That's the right attitude if you're offering a guarantee.

Similarly, customers should not be made to feel guilty about invoking the guarantee – no questioning, no raised eyebrows, or "Why me, Lord?" looks. A company should encourage unhappy customers to invoke its guarantee, not put up roadblocks to keep them from speaking up.

Easy to Collect. Customers shouldn't have to work hard to collect a payout, either. The procedure should be easy and, equally important, quick – on the spot, if possible. Dissatisfaction with a Manpower temporary worker, for instance, results in an immediate credit to your bill.

What you should *not* do in your guarantee: don't promise something your customers already expect; don't shroud a guarantee in so many conditions that it loses its point; and don't offer a guarantee so mild

---

1. See British Airways study cited in Karl Albrecht and Ron Zemke, *Service America!* (Homewood, Ill.: Dow Jones-Irwin, 1985), pp. 33-34.

that it is never invoked. A guarantee that is essentially risk free to the company will be of little or no value to your customers—and may be a joke to your employees.

Why a Service Guarantee Works

A guarantee is a powerful tool—both for marketing service quality and for achieving it—for five reasons.

First, it pushes the entire company to focus on customers' definition of good service—not on executives' assumptions. Second, it sets clear performance standards, which boost employee performance and morale. Third, it generates reliable data (through payouts) when performance is poor. Fourth, it forces an organization to examine its entire service-delivery system for possible failure points. Last, it builds customer loyalty, sales, and market share.

A guarantee forces you to focus on customers. Knowing what customers want is the sine qua non in offering a service guarantee. A company has to identify its target customers' expectations about the elements of the service and the importance they attach to each. Lacking this knowledge of customer needs, a company that wants to guarantee its service may very well guarantee the wrong things.

British Airways conducted a market study and found that its passengers judge its customer services on four dimensions:[1]

1. Care and concern (employees' friendliness, courtesy, and warmth).

2. Initiative (employees' ability and willingness to jockey the system on the customer's behalf).

3. Problem solving (figuring out solutions to customer problems, whether unusual or routine—like multiflight airline tickets).

4. Recovery (going the extra yard, when things go wrong, to handle a particular problem—which includes the simple but often overlooked step of delivering an apology).

British Airways managers confessed that they hadn't even thought about the second and fourth categories. Worse, they realized that if *they* hadn't understood these important dimensions of customer service, how much thought could their employees be giving to them?

A guarantee sets clear standards. A specific, unambiguous service guarantee sets standards for your organization. It tells employees what the company stands for. BBBK stands for pest elimination, not pest control; Federal Express stands for "absolutely, positively by 10:30 A.M.," not "sometime tomorrow, probably." And it forces the company to define each

employee's role and responsibilities in delivering the service. Salespeople, for example, know precisely what their companies can deliver and can represent that accurately—the opposite of the common situation in which salespeople promise the moon and customers get only dirt.

This clarity and sense of identity have the added advantage of creating employee team spirit and pride. Mitchell Fromstein, president and CEO of Manpower, says, "At one point, we wondered what the marketing impact would be if we dropped our guarantee. We figured that our accounts were well aware of the guarantee and that it might not have much marketing power anymore. Our employees' reaction was fierce—and it had a lot less to do with marketing than with the pride they take in their work. They said, 'The guarantee is proof that we're a great company. We're willing to tell our customers that if they don't like our service for any reason, it's our fault, not

A service guarantee is valued when a customer's ego is on the line.

theirs, and we'll make it right.' I realized then that the guarantee is far more than a simple piece of paper that puts customers at ease. It really sets the tone, externally and, perhaps more important, internally, for our commitment to our customers and workers."

A payout that creates financial pain when errors occur is also a powerful statement, to employees and customers alike, that management demands customer satisfaction. A significant payout ensures that both middle and upper management will take the service guarantee seriously; it provides a strong incentive to take every step necessary to deliver. A manager who must bear the full cost of mistakes has ample incentive to figure out how to prevent them from happening.

A guarantee generates feedback. A guarantee creates the goal; it defines what you must do to satisfy your customers. Next, you need to know when you go wrong. A guarantee forces you to create a system for discovering errors—which the Japanese call "golden nuggets" because they're opportunities to learn.

Arguably the greatest ailment afflicting service companies is a lack of decent systems for generating and acting on customer data. Dissatisfied service customers have little incentive to complain on their own, far less so than unhappy product owners do. Many elements of a service are intangible, so consumers who receive poor service are often left with no evidence to support their complaints. (The customer believes the waiter was rude; perhaps the waiter will deny it.) Second, without the equivalent of a product warranty, customers don't know their rights. (Is 15 minutes too long to wait for a restaurant meal? 30 minutes?) Third, there is often no one to complain to—at least no one who looks capable of

> **Without a guarantee, customers won't complain. Or come back.**

solving the problem. Often, complaining directly to the person who is rendering poor service will only make things worse.

Customer comment cards have traditionally been the most common method of gathering customer feedback on a company's operations, but they, too, are inadequate for collecting valid, reliable error data. In the first place, they are an impersonal form of communication and are usually short (to maximize the response rate). Why bother, people think, to cram the details of a bad experience onto a printed survey form with a handful of "excellent—good—fair" check-off boxes? Few aggrieved customers believe that com-

pleting a comment card will resolve their problems. Therefore, only a few customers—usually the most satisfied and dissatisfied—provide feedback through such forms, and fewer still provide meaningful feedback. As a broad gauge of customer sentiment, cards and surveys are useful, but for specific information about customer problems and operational weaknesses, they simply don't fill the bill.

Service companies thus have a hard time collecting error data. Less information on mistakes means fewer opportunities to improve, ultimately resulting in more service errors and more customer dissatisfaction—a cycle that management is often unaware of. A guarantee attacks this malady by giving consumers an incentive and a vehicle for bringing their grievances to management's attention.

Manpower uses its guarantee to glean error data in addition to allaying customer worries about using an unknown quantity (the temporary worker). Every customer who employs a Manpower temporary worker is called the first day of a one-day assignment or the second day of a longer assignment to check on the worker's performance. A dissatisfied customer doesn't pay—period. (Manpower pays the worker, however; it assumes complete responsibility for the quality of its service.) The company uses its error data to improve both its work force and its proprietary skills-testing software and skills data base—major elements in its ability to match worker skills to customer requirements. The information Manpower obtains before and after hiring enables it to offer its guarantee with confidence.

A guarantee forces you to understand why you fail. In developing a guarantee, managers must ask questions like these: What failure points exist in the system? If failure points can be identified, can their origins be traced—and overcome? A company that wants to promise timely service delivery, for example, must first understand its operation's capability and the factors limiting that capability. Many service executives, lacking understanding of such basic issues as system throughput time, capacity, and process flow, tend to blame workers, customers, or anything *but* the service-delivery process.

Even if workers *are* a problem, managers can do several things to "fix" the organization so that it can support a guarantee—such as design better recruiting, hiring, and training processes. The pest-control industry has historically suffered from unmotivated personnel and high turnover. Al Burger overcame the status quo by offering higher than average pay (attracting a higher caliber of job candidate), using a vigorous screening program (making those hired feel like members of a select group), training all workers for six months, and keeping them motivated by giving them a great deal of autonomy and lots of recognition.

Some managers may be unwilling to pay for an internal service-delivery capability that is above the industry average. Fine. They will never have better than average organizations, either, and they will

A guarantee uncovers errors — and opportunities to learn.

therefore never be able to develop the kind of competitive advantage that flows from a good service guarantee.

A guarantee builds marketing muscle. Perhaps the most obvious reason for offering a strong service guarantee is its ability to boost marketing: it encourages consumers to buy a service by reducing the risk of the purchase decision, and it generates more sales to existing customers by enhancing loyalty. In the last ten years, Manpower's revenues have mushroomed from $400 million to $4 billion. That's marketing impact.

Keeping most of your customers and getting positive word of mouth, though desirable in any business, are particularly important for service companies. The net present value of sales forgone from lost customers—in other words, the cost of customer dissatisfaction—is enormous. In this respect, it's fair to say that many service companies' biggest competitors are themselves. They frequently spend huge amounts of money to attract new customers without ever figuring out how to provide the consistent service they promise to their existing customers. If customers aren't satisfied, the marketing money has been poured down the drain and may even engender further ill will. (See the insert, "Maximizing Marketing Impact.")

A guarantee will only work, of course, if you start with commitment to the customer. If your aim is to minimize the guarantee's impact on your organization but to maximize its marketing punch, you won't succeed. In the long run, you will nullify the guarantee's potential impact on customers, and your marketing dollars will go down the drain.

Phil Bressler, owner of 18 Domino's Pizza franchises in the Baltimore, Maryland area, demonstrates the right commitment to customers. He got upset the time his company recorded its highest monthly earnings ever because, he correctly figured, the profits had come from money that should have been paid out on the Domino's guarantee of "delivery within 30 minutes or $3 off." Bressler's unit managers,

who have bottom-line responsibility, had pumped up their short-term profits by failing to honor the guarantee consistently. Bressler is convinced that money spent on guarantees is an investment in customer satisfaction and loyalty. He also recognizes that the guarantee is the best way to identify weak operations, and that guarantees not acted on are data not collected.

Compare Bressler's attitude with that of an owner of several nationally franchised motels. *His* guarantee promises that the company will do "everything possible" to remedy a customer's problem; if the problem cannot be resolved, the customer stays for free. He brags that he's paid, on average, refunds for only two room guarantees per motel per year—a minuscule percentage of room sales. "If my managers are doing their jobs, I don't have to pay out for the guarantee," he says. "If I do have to pay out, my managers are not doing their jobs, and I get rid of them."

Clearly, more than two guests of *any* hotel are likely to be dissatisfied over the course of a year. By seeking to limit payouts rather than hear complaints, this owner is undoubtedly blowing countless opportunities to create loyal customers out of disgruntled ones. He is also losing rich information about which of his motels need improvement and why, information that can most easily be obtained from customer complaints. You have to wonder why he offers a guarantee at all, since he completely misses the point.

Why You May Need a Guarantee Even If You Don't Think So

Of course, guarantees may not be effective or practicable for all service firms. Four Seasons Hotels, for example, could probably not get much marketing or operational mileage from a guarantee. With its strong internal vision of absolute customer satisfaction, the company has developed an outstanding service-delivery system and a reputation to match. Thus it already has an implicit guarantee. To advertise the obvious would produce little gain and might actually be perceived as incongruent with the company's prestigious image.

A crucial element in Four Seasons's service strategy is instilling in all employees a mission of absolute customer satisfaction and empowering them to do whatever is necessary if customer problems do occur. For example, Four Seasons's Washington hotel was once asked by the State Department to make room for a foreign dignitary. Already booked to capacity, Four Seasons had to tell four other customers

Maximizing Marketing Impact

The odds of gaining powerful marketing impact from a service guarantee are in your favor when one or more of the following conditions exist:

The price of the service is high. A bad shoe shine? No big deal. A botched $1,000 car repair is a different story; a guarantee is more effective here.

The customer's ego is on the line. Who wants to be seen after getting a bad haircut?

The customer's expertise with the service is low. When in doubt about a service, a customer will choose one that's covered by a guarantee over those that are not.

The negative consequences of service failure are high. As consumers' expected aggravation, expense, and time lost due to service failure increase, a guarantee gains power. Your computer went down? A computer-repair service with guaranteed response and repair times would be the most logical company to call.

The industry has a bad image for service quality – like pest-control services, security guards, or home repair. A guard company that guarantees to have its posts filled by qualified people would automatically rank high on a list of prospective vendors.

The company depends on frequent customer repurchases. Can it exist on a never-ending stream of new triers (like small service businesses in large markets), or does it have to deal with a finite market? If the market is finite, how close is market saturation? The smaller the size of the potential market of new triers, the more attention management should pay to increasing the loyalty and repurchase rate of existing customers – objectives that a good service guarantee will serve.

The company's business is affected deeply by word of mouth (both positive and negative). Consultants, stockbrokers, restaurants, and resorts are all good examples of services where there are strong incentives to minimize the extent of customer dissatisfaction – and hence, negative word of mouth.

with reservations that they could not be accommodated. However, the hotel immediately found rooms for them at another first-class hotel, while assuring them they would remain registered at the Four Seasons (so that any messages they received would be taken and sent to the other hotel). When rooms became available, the customers were driven back to the Four Seasons by limousine. Four Seasons also paid for their rooms at the other hotel. It was the equivalent of a full money-back guarantee, and more.

Does this mean that every company that performs at the level of a Four Seasons need not offer a service guarantee? Could Federal Express, for example, drop its "absolutely, positively" assurance with little or no effect? Probably not. Its guarantee is such a part of its image that dropping the guarantee would hurt it.

In general, organizations that meet the following tests probably have little to gain by offering a service guarantee: the company is perceived by the market to be the quality leader in its industry; every employee is inculcated with the "absolute customer satisfaction" philosophy; employees are empowered to take whatever corrective action is necessary to handle complaints; errors are few; and a stated guarantee would be at odds with the company's image.

It is probably unnecessary to point out that few service companies meet these tests.

External Variables. Service guarantees may also be impractical where customer satisfaction is influenced strongly by external forces the service provider can't control. While everybody thinks their businesses are in this fix, most are wrong.

How many variables are truly beyond management's control? Not the work force. Not equipment

> ## An airline can't guarantee on-time flights – but it *can* promise courtesy.

problems. Not vendor quality. And even businesses subject to "acts of God" (like weather) can control a great deal of their service quality.

BBBK is an example of how one company turned the situation around by analyzing the elements of the service-delivery process. By asking, "What obstacles stand in the way of our guaranteeing pest elimination?" Al Burger discovered that clients' poor cleaning and storage practices were one such obstacle. So the company requires customers to maintain sanitary practices and in some cases even make physical changes to their property (like putting in walls). By changing the process, the company could guarantee the outcome.

There may well be uncontrollable factors that create problems. As I noted earlier, such things as flight controllers, airport capacity, and weather limit the extent to which even the finest airline can consistently deliver on-time service. But how employees respond to such externally imposed problems strongly influences customer satisfaction, as British Airways executives learned from their market survey. When things go wrong, will employees go the extra yard to handle the problem? Why couldn't an airline that has refined its problem-handling skills to a science ensure absolute customer satisfaction—uncontrollable variables be damned? How many customers would invoke a guarantee if they understood that the reasons for a problem were completely out of the airline's control—if they were treated with warmth, compassion, and a sense of humor, and if the airline's staff communicated with them honestly?

Cheating. Fear of customer cheating is another big hurdle for most service managers considering offer-

> ## A guarantee can generate breakthrough service and change an industry.

ing guarantees. When asked why Lufthansa's guarantee required customers to present written proof of purchase, a manager at the airline's U.S. headquarters told me, "If we didn't ask for written proof, our customers would cheat us blind."

But experience teaches a different lesson. Sure, there will be cheats—the handful of customers who take advantage of a guarantee to get something for nothing. What they cost the company amounts to very little compared to the benefits derived from a strong guarantee. Says Michael Leven, a hotel industry executive, "Too often management spends its time worrying about the 1% of people who might cheat the company instead of the 99% who don't."

Phil Bressler of Domino's argues that customers cheat only when *they* feel cheated: "If we charge $8 for a pizza, our customers expect $8 worth of product and service. If we started giving them $7.50 worth of product and service, then they'd start looking for ways to get back that extra 50 cents. Companies create the incentive to cheat, in almost all cases, by cutting costs and not providing value."

Where the potential for false claims is high, a no-questions-asked guarantee may appear to be foolhardy. When Domino's first offered its "delivery within 30 minutes or the pizza is free" guarantee, some college students telephoned orders from hard-to-find locations. The result was free pizza for the students and lost revenue for Domino's. In this environment, the guarantee was problematic because some students perceived it as a game against Domino's. But Bressler takes the view that the revenue thus lost was an investment in the future. "They'll be Domino's customers for life, those kids," he says.

High Costs. Managers are likely to worry about the costs of a service-guarantee program, but for the wrong reasons. Quality "guru" Philip Crosby coined the phrase "quality is free" (in his 1979 book, *Quality Is Free*) to indicate *not* that quality-improvement efforts cost nothing but that the benefits of quality improvement—fewer errors, higher productivity, more repeat business—outweigh the costs over the long term.

Clearly, a company whose operations are slipshod (or out of control) should not consider offering an unconditional guarantee; the outcome would be either bankruptcy from staggering payouts or an employee revolt stemming from demands to meet standards that are beyond the organization's capability. If your company is like most, however, it's not in that shape; you will probably only need to buttress operations somewhat. To be sure, an investment of financial and human resources to shore up weak points in the delivery system will likely cause a quick, sharp rise in expenditures.

How sharp an increase depends on several factors: your company's weaknesses (how far does it have to go to become good?), the nature of the industry, and the strength of your competition, for example. A small restaurant might simply spend more on employee recruiting and training, and perhaps on sponsoring quality circles; a large utility company might need to restructure its entire organization to overcome years of bad habits if it is to deliver on a guarantee.

Even though a guarantee carries costs, bear in mind that, as Crosby asserts, a badly performed service also incurs costs—failure costs, which come in many forms, including lost business from disgruntled consumers. In a guarantee program, you shift from spending to mop up failures to spending on preventing failures. And many of those costs are incurred in most organizations anyway (like outlays for staff time spent in planning meetings). It's just that they're spent more productively.

Breakthrough Service

One great potential of a service guarantee is its ability to change an industry's rules of the game by changing the service-delivery process as competitors conceive it.

BBBK and Federal Express both redefined the meaning of service in their industries, performing at levels that other companies have so far been unable to match. (According to the owner of a competing pest-control company, BBBK "is number one. There is no number two.") By offering breakthrough service, these companies altered the basis of competition in their businesses and put their competitors at a severe disadvantage.

What are the possibilities for replicating their success in other service businesses? Skeptics might claim that BBBK's and Federal Express's success is not widely applicable because they target price-insensitive customers willing to pay for superior service – in short, that these companies are pursuing differentiation strategies.

It is true that BBBK's complex preparation, cleaning, and checkup procedures are much more time consuming than those of typical pest-control operators, that the company spends more on pesticides than competitors do, and that its employees are well compensated. And many restaurants and hotels are willing to pay BBBK's higher prices because to them it's ultimately cheaper: the cost of "errors" (guests' spotting roaches or ants) is higher than the cost of error prevention.

But, because of the "quality is free" dictum, breakthrough service does not mean you must become the high-cost producer. Manpower's procedures are not radically more expensive than its competitors';

Author's note: I thank Dan Maher for assistance in researching and writing this article.

they're simply better. The company's skills-testing methods and customer-needs diagnoses surely cost less in the long run than a sloppy system. A company that inadequately screens and trains temporary-worker recruits, establishes no detailed customer specifications, and fails to check worker performance loses customers.

Manpower spends heavily on ways to reduce errors further, seeing this spending as an investment that will (a) protect its market position; (b) reduce time-consuming service errors; and (c) reinforce the company's values to employees. Here is the "absolute customer satisfaction" philosophy at work, and whatever cost increase Manpower incurs it makes up in sales volume.

Organizations that figure out how to offer – and deliver – guaranteed, breakthrough service will have tapped into a powerful source of competitive advantage. Doing so is no mean feat, of course, which is precisely why the opportunity to build a competitive advantage exists. Though the task is difficult, it is clearly not impossible, and the service guarantee can play a fundamental role in the process.　　▽

Reprint 88405

*"Actually, I don't want to make a deposit or a withdrawal
I just wanted to make sure everything was, you know, fine."*

The key to growth and profits is getting employees to give away more of your products and services.

My Employees Are My Service Guarantee

by Timothy W. Firnstahl

I own a chain of four restaurants in and around Seattle, and my company exists for one reason only – to make other people happy. Every time a customer leaves one of our restaurants with a more optimistic view of the world, we've done our job. Every time we fail to raise a customer's spirits with good food, gratifying service, and a soothing atmosphere, we haven't done our job.

To the extent that we satisfy customers, we fulfill our company goal. This observation may seem self-evident and trivial – a useful motto, a business axiom that a lot of business-people understandably overlook in the day-to-day flood of details – but I have found it the very key to growth and profits. And after much trial and error, I have come up with a strategy for ensuring customer satisfaction that has worked wonders in our business and can, I'm convinced, work wonders in other businesses as well.

It starts with a guarantee – not that moth-eaten old promise of a cheerful refund – but a guarantee that customers will be satisfied with their whole experience of the company's products and services. It moves on to a system for giving employees complete responsibility and *authority* for making the guarantee stick. It ends with a process for identifying system failures – the problems in organization, training, and other internal programs that cause customer dissatisfaction.

I call the whole thing "ultimate strategy." That may sound pretentious. But because it redefines a company's ultimate reason for being and succeeding, and because it underlines the importance of finding the ultimate causes of every system failure, I think the name is justified.

Service with a smile and a seed of doubt

Ultimate strategy had its origins in the success of a restaurant business I cofounded ten years ago. (I recently started a different restaurant business, but the strategy hasn't changed.) The first restaurant, specializing in steaks and featuring a huge bar, went over so well that we opened another. Five years ago, we had three restaurants, $7.5 million in sales, and moderate profits. Clearly, many of our customers were satisfied.

But I was bothered by what I saw as an unacceptable level of complaints and by our haphazard responses to them. Not that we didn't try. We happily apologized and gave a free dessert to any customer who complained about slow service, and we cheerfully picked up the cleaning bill when one of our employees spilled the soup. Customers who wrote in to complain about reservations mix-ups or rude service got certificates for complimentary meals.

It was just that our procedures for responding seemed all wrong. Giving out that free dessert required approval from a manager. Getting a suit cleaned meant filling out a form and getting a manager to sign it. I also didn't like the idea that people had to write us with their complaints before we made amends. And I wasn't convinced that a free meal was enough.

Moreover, our response to complaints didn't appear to have any effect on the number or type of complaints we received, most of which concerned speed of service and quality of food. And it wasn't the employees' fault. They knew complaints had top priority, but they didn't know how to respond to them. We were all on a treadmill, getting nowhere.

The guarantee

Then five years ago, when the book *In Search of Excellence* was in vogue, I spent considerable time writing Ten Tenets of Excellence for our organization. We included them in our train-

Founder and CEO of Satisfaction Guaranteed Eateries, Inc. in Seattle, Timothy W. Firnstahl is a restaurant zealot and the fourth generation of his family in the food industry. Previously, he wrote for HBR on how entrepreneurs can delegate responsibility.

ing manuals and posted them in the restaurants and the offices. One day about a year later, someone asked me what the sixth tenet was, and I couldn't tell her. It came to me that if I couldn't remember the Ten Tenets of Excellence, surely no one else could either. That meant the company had no strategy known to its employees.

So I hit on something simpler and more compelling – the guarantee. We expressed it as a promise: *Your Enjoyment Guaranteed. Always.* As a company rallying cry, it seemed to work much better than the Tenets of Excellence. Cryptic mission statements, unreviewed strategic plans, the hidden dreams of management: all that gave way to a company game plan – customer satisfaction – that everyone could understand and remember and act on. For the first time, employees and management had a strategy in common.

Your Enjoyment Guaranteed. Always. This promise became our driving force. We included it in all our advertising. We printed it on every menu, letterhead, and guest check. To make it live for our employees, we did a series of internal promotions. We reduced it to an acronym, YEGA, and posted it everywhere for employees to see.

What good is a guarantee that makes complaining an ordeal for the customer?

We held a series of meetings, where we found workers receptive to both the acronym and the simplicity of the idea. Each of our 600 employees signed a contract pledging YEGA follow-through. We created a YEGA logo and put it everywhere, on report forms, on training manuals, on wall signs. We started the *YEGA News* and distributed YEGA pins, shirts, name tags, even underwear. We announced that failure to enforce YEGA would be cause for dismissal.

For a year or so, YEGA dominated the company's consciousness. But as time went by, I grew increasingly uncomfortable. Complaints were coming in at the same old rate. I could see the guarantee being implemented here and there, now and then, but not on a regular, companywide basis. I'd run into another brick wall.

Empowering employees

One evening about two years back as I was driving home from work, the cause of the problem hit me. The guarantee by itself wasn't enough. We had given employees responsibility without giving them authority. The result was that they tried to bury mistakes or blame others. I saw it every time we tried to track down a complaint. The food servers blamed the kitchen for late meals. The kitchen blamed the food servers for placing orders incorrectly.

Problems inevitably crop up in a busy restaurant, and when a customer grumbles the tendency is to gloss over the complaint with pleasantness. Follow-through means fetching the manager or filling out forms or both. Climbing the ladder of hierarchical approvals is simply too frustrating and time-consuming – for customer as well as employee.

For our guarantee to be truly effective, we needed to give workers themselves the power to make good on the promise of the guarantee – at once and on the spot. Eliminate the hassle for the customer and for ourselves. No forms to fill out, no phone calls to make, no 40 questions to answer, just immediate redress by the closest employee.

So I instituted the idea that employees could and should do *anything* to keep the customer happy. In the event of an error or delay, any employee right down to the busboy could provide complimentary wine or desserts, or pick up an entire tab if necessary.

Of course, we provided some guidelines. For instance, when guests have to wait more than 10 minutes beyond their reservation time, but less than 20, we suggest free drinks. If they wait more than 20 minutes, the entire meal might be free. If the bread arrives more than 5 minutes after

the guests sit down, we suggest free clam chowder. And so forth, using what we know to be optimum intervals for most orders.

At the same time, we urged employees not to get bogged down in the guidelines. The last thing we wanted was nitpicking: "OK, I got them the bread in five minutes exactly. Do I just apologize, or do they get clam chowder?" Satisfaction does not mean quibbling – it means a contented customer. Different guests respond in different ways, so we told our employees not to feel limited by the guidelines and to do whatever it took to make sure guests enjoyed themselves.

Employees were initially wary of their new authority. Never having had complete control, they were naturally hesitant and skeptical. It was hard to convince them they wouldn't be penalized for giving away free food and drinks.

But once they got used to the idea, employees liked knowing that the company believed so strongly in its products and services that it wholeheartedly stood behind its work – and theirs. They liked working for a restaurant known for its unhesitating commitment to customer satisfaction. Preeminence in any field gives people feelings of self-worth they could never get from just making a buck. Their power as company representatives increased their pride in the business, and that, in turn, increased motivation.

Once our employees overcame their skepticism, they quickly grew creative and aggressive in their approach to the guarantee. In one case, a customer wanted a margarita made the way a competitor made its. So our bartender called the bartender at the other restaurant and, bartender-to-bartender, learned the special recipe. In another case, an elderly woman who had not been in our restaurant for years ordered breakfast, which we no longer served. The waiter and the chef sent someone to the market for bacon and eggs and served the breakfast she wanted.

If the guarantee is really working the way it's supposed to, customers become less inhibited about complaining. Too often, customers hold their peace but vote with their feet by taking their business to the competition. The promise of the guarantee's enforcement stimulates them to help us expose our own failures.

We even asked for their criticism. Once a month, using reservations lists and credit card charges, groups of employees called several hundred customers and asked them to rate their experience. Were the food and service lousy, OK, good, very good, or excellent? If they said "OK," that meant "lousy" to us, and they got a letter of apology, a certificate for a free meal, and a follow-up phone call.

Aside from the data we gathered, the phone calls were great promotion. Most people were amazed and delighted that we took the trouble to phone them, and many developed enormous loyalty to our restaurants.

System-failure costs

Customer complaints are company failures and require immediate correction. So far so good. But corrections cost money. Free drinks and meals add up quickly.

Yet, paradoxically, spending money is the goal. Every dollar paid out to offset customer dissatisfaction is a signal that the company must change in some decisive way. The guarantee brings out a true, hard-dollars picture of company failures and forces us to assume full responsibility for our output. The cost of keeping a company's promises is not just the price tag on the guarantee, it is the cost of system failure. The money was spent because the product did not perform, and when the product fails to perform, the system that produced it is at fault.

A somnolent business can be rudely awakened by the magnitude of its system-failure costs. We certainly were. Our previous guarantee expenses doubled. The problems had always been there, hidden. Only the huge cost of the new strategy revealed that they were gutting profits. Suddenly, we had a real incentive to fix the systems that weren't working, since the alternatives—sacrificing profits permanently or restricting the power to enforce the guarantee—were both unacceptable.

> ## Every dollar you give away is a plus—it puts your finger on a problem you can fix.

Notice that system-failure costs are not the same as employee-failure costs. System-failure costs measure the extent of the confusion in company structure, for which management alone is to blame. By welcoming every guarantee payoff—every system-failure expense—as an otherwise lost insight, you can make every problem pay a dividend. The trick is to reject Band-Aid solutions, to insist on finding the ultimate cause of each problem, and then to demand and expect decisive change. (Another way to sugarcoat the pill of system-failure costs is to think of the free food and drinks as a word-of-mouth advertising budget. No one forgets to mention a free meal to a friend or neighbor.)

Our search for the culprit in a string of complaints about slow food service in one restaurant led first to the kitchen and then to one cook. But pushing the search one step further revealed several unrealistically complex dishes that no one could have prepared swiftly.

In another case, our kitchens were turning out wrong orders at a rate

---

The Hassle Factor

Imagine you've bought a new pair of shoes at a downtown store. A week later, one sole starts to come off, so you take them back. You drive downtown through heavy traffic and spend 15 minutes finding a parking place. You explain the problem to the salesman, who says, "We stand behind our merchandise." He gives you a new pair of shoes.

Question One: Are you happy?

Answer: Well, no, you're not. Sure, you got a new pair of shoes, and the salesman was pleasant enough, but you had to take time out of your day and go to a lot of trouble to get what you should have gotten in the first place. In short, the whole transaction was a hassle, and neither the salesman nor the store did anything to make it up to you.

Question Two: What should they have done?

Answer: Replace plus one. Besides giving you a new pair of shoes, the salesman should have thrown in a pair of socks or stockings to repay you for your hassle. Instead of, "We'll replace inferior merchandise whenever a customer complains," the store's message should be, "We really regret your inconvenience and want to make you happy."

Like the shoe store, we stand behind our products and services. Unlike the shoe store, we'll do more than the customer demands to make it right. If a guest doesn't like her salad, don't charge her for it. But what about the Hassle Factor?

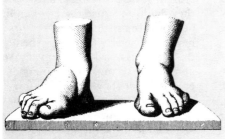

Replace plus one. By all means, give her the salad free of charge. But buy her a drink or dessert as well—or whatever else it takes to make her happy.

Adapted from the restaurant training manual

that was costing us thousands of dollars a month in wasted food. The cooks insisted that the food servers were punching incorrect orders into the kitchen printout computer. In times past, we might have ended our search right there, accused the food servers of sloppiness, and asked everyone to be more careful. But now, adhering to the principle of system failure not people failure, we looked beyond the symptoms and found a flaw in our training. We had simply never taught food servers to double-check their orders on the computer screen, and the system offered no reward for doing so. Mistakes plummeted as soon as we started training people properly and handing out awards each month for the fewest ordering errors and posting lists of the worst offenders (no punishments, just names).

Of course, correcting system failures is seldom an easy task. One way to avoid making problems worse is to audition problem solutions with small, quick-hit field tests. For exam-

> ## What is a word-of-mouth advertising budget? It's the money you spend honoring your guarantee.

ple, we experimented with new service procedures at one station in one restaurant, or we offered new menu items as nonmenu specials, or we borrowed equipment for a test run before leasing or buying it. When we had a problem with coffee quality, we tried using expensive, high-quality vacuum carafes in one restaurant. Quality improved substantially (and waste was cut in half), so we adopted the thermoses in all our restaurants.

When some customers complained about our wine service, we realized that we gave the subject only

1. For more on guarantees, see Christopher W. L. Hart, "The Power of Unconditional Service Guarantees," HBR July-August 1988, p. 54.

three pages in our employee manual. So we put together a training and motivation package that included instruction about the characteristics and distinctions of different wines, as well as a system of awards for selling them effectively. We also pointed out to our food servers that selling more wine increases the size of checks and thus of tips.

In short, honoring the guarantee has led to new training procedures, recipe and menu changes, restaurant redesign, equipment purchases, and whatever else it took to put things right and keep them right. In the long run, the guarantee works only if it reduces system-failure costs and increases customer satisfaction.[1]

This kind of problem solving is popular with employees. Since the object of change is always the company, employees don't get blamed for problems beyond their control.

As you find and correct the ultimate causes of your system failures, you can reasonably expect your profits to improve. But you can begin to tell if you're succeeding even before you see it on the bottom line. Remember, costs will go up before they come down, so high system-failure costs and low phone-survey complaint rates probably mean you're on the right track. Conversely, low system-failure costs and a high rate of "lousies" and "OKs" from customers almost certainly indicate that the promise is not being kept, that your expensive system failures are not getting corrected, and that your organization has yet to understand that customer satisfaction is the only reason for the company's existence.

Our own system-failure costs rose to a high of $40,000 a month two years ago and then fell to $10,000 a month. Meanwhile, sales rose 25%, profits doubled, and the cash in the bank grew two-and-a-half times.

Making it work

It is easier to give someone a bowl of clam chowder than a free CAT scanner or an industry marketing study, so of course the nature of the guarantee will change from business to business. Still, the point is not free food, the point is customer satisfac-

tion. It is always possible to satisfy the customer if the business is sufficiently committed to that goal.

Here are my suggestions for formulating your own ultimate strategy.

1. *Make the guarantee simple and easy to understand.* Think about the company's primary customer benefit

> ## Firnstahl's first rule: Always deal with complaints before they're made.

and how you achieve it. In our case, the principal benefit is enjoyment. For many, it will be dependability. For others, cost or flexibility.

For the sake of impact, try to develop a guarantee that's memorable, maybe one that reduces to an acronym. The restaurants I now own use WAGS (We Always Guarantee Satisfaction), which I like even better than YEGA. Whatever you do, make it significant, simple, and unconditional. Think of these famous promises that changed whole companies:

"We try harder." (Avis)

"Absolutely Positively Overnight." (Federal Express)

Once you settle on a guarantee, commit to it for the long term. Continual change confuses the public and the organization. Plan to stick with a particular promise for at least five years.

2. *Make sure employees know how to use their new authority.* For most employees, full power and responsibility to put things right will be a new experience. After all, they're used to the old hierarchical approach. So it's up to you to make sure they don't underuse their power. In our training programs, we advise new employees to take action before the guest has to ask for a remedy. We don't want to make customers decide whether they're entitled to get something free–most people find that embarrassing. The food server should find the solution and present it to the guest as a done deal: "I'm sorry your drink wasn't prepared the

way you like it. Of course, there will be no charge for that. And please accept these chowders on the house with my apologies."

We also insist that the customer is always right, even when the customer is wrong. Let's say a guest insists that all clam chowder has

---

Giving your employees total power and authority will scare them to death and make you rich.

---

potatoes. He's wrong, but that's no excuse to make him look stupid. When we say, "The guest is never wrong," we mean a server should never question a guest's judgment and perception. Don't stand and argue about whether a steak is medium-rare or medium. Take it away and get one broiled the way the customer wants it.

The real issues are these: The guest is there to have a good time. The guest is in the employee's care.

Finally, we think that power and responsibility are not enough. Employees must also have rewards. Good thinking and positive action deserve money, praise, the limelight, advancement, and all the other encouragements a company can think of.

We spark employee thought and action by dividing a $10,000 bonus among the employees of each restaurant once its system-failure costs and phone-audit complaint rates drop to 25% of their all-time highs. Every month, we pay thousands of dollars in awards to employees who have helped to find and cure the ultimate causes of system failures. In effect, we commission everyone to change the organization for the better.

3. *Make progress visible.* Stay away from written progress reports — graphs communicate better. A creative in-house accountant can play with the data until it's readily under-

standable to everyone. We display our new WAGS graphics throughout the company for everyone to see.

In our experience, system-failure costs go through four phases.

Start: Employees are wary of using their new power and authority. Phone-audit complaint rates are high and system-failure costs are low.

Under way: Employees begin to believe in the organization's commitment to the guarantee. Phone-audit complaint rates are still high; system-failure costs start to rise.

Mid-point: Employees accept and act on the company promise. System-failure costs remain high. Phone-audit complaint rates start dropping as the company starts satisfying customers in earnest.

Success: The company has achieved elemental change and raised itself to a higher level of merit. System-failure costs and phone-audit complaint rates are both low.

In general, there is a roller coaster effect that tells you when ultimate strategy is working. Costs go up. Complaints go down. Sales go up. Costs go down. Profits go up.

One word of caution: you will never perfect your company's system. As long as you offer an absolute guarantee on your products and services, you will incur system-failure costs. There is always more work to do, and a CEO's personal commitment and persistence are often necessary to get it done. But motivated employees are essential.

People often ask us where we find such wonderful employees. While it's true that we screen carefully, I believe our employees are better than most because they have the power and the obligation to solve customer problems on their own and on the spot. Giving them complete discretion about how they do it has also given them pride. Many companies have tried so many different programs and gimmicks that employees have become cynical and indifferent. The people who work for us know we take our guarantee seriously — and expect them to do the same. We use the same ultimate strategy to satisfy both customers and employees.

Reprint 89407

A variety of strategies, like equipment loans during downtimes and fast service response, is necessary to get and hold customers

Good product support is smart marketing

Milind M. Lele and Uday S. Karmarkar

Product support can be as simple as a set of instructions and a throwaway wrench that comes with an assemble-it-yourself child's bicycle or as complicated as warranty programs, service contracts, parts depots, and equipment on loan to replace a defective machine while it is being repaired. All of these constitute product support; they are designed to ensure that customers obtain the most value from use of the product after the sale. Such factors as heightened customer awareness and higher expectations about support levels, reduced ability to perceive product differentiation through superior technology and/ or features, and improvements in support methodology have greatly increased the importance of product support in company strategy. The identification of customer expectations regarding product support and the development of cost-effective strategies for meeting those expectations is, these authors demonstrate, a major facet of successful marketing today.

Mr. Lele is the managing director of Lele & Company, a management consulting firm based in Evanston, Illinois, and visiting professor of marketing at the Kellogg Graduate School of Management, Northwestern University. He has worked for the past 13 years with a number of large U.S. and overseas clients on problems of industrial marketing, operations, and business strategy. Mr. Karmarkar is associate professor and area coordinator of operations management and operations research at the Graduate School of Management, University of Rochester. His research interests include production scheduling, product support, inventory theory, and decision behavior.

When making purchases, customers often believe they are buying more than the physical item; they also have expectations about the level of postpurchase support the product carries with it. This support can range from simple replacement of a faulty item to complex arrangements designed to meet customer needs over the product's entire useful life. Our investigations show that defining these expectations of support and meeting them effectively can be critical to a successful marketing effort. Consider:

☐ Caterpillar Tractor and John Deere, two companies whose marketing strategies are based on providing superior product support. Over the past quarter century both have concentrated on strengthening their dealers' service capabilities and on upgrading parts availability. They have backed these efforts with extensive service staffs and emergency parts ordering systems. They have directed equipment design to emphasize reliability and serviceability, and to minimize downtime. These two companies have made product support cornerstones of their organizations' corporate cultures and values.[1] This has remained true despite damaging strikes, recession, and acreage taken out of production.

☐ The failure of Olivetti to establish itself in the United States, despite considerable investment during the past 15 years, primarily because of poor product support. The company has vacillated in its choice of distribution channels, thereby demoralizing its dealers. Parts and service training support have been inconsistent and usually poor. Initial buyer enthusiasm for new products has been repeatedly dampened by inadequate documentation and user

1 Thomas J. Peters and Robert H. Waterman, Jr., *In Search of Excellence: Lessons from America's Best-Run Companies* (New York: Harper & Row, 1982) and "How Deere Outclasses the Competition," *Forbes,* January 21, 1980, p. 79.

training. As a result, despite excellent products at competitive prices, the company has failed to gain a strong foothold in the U.S. market.

Caterpillar and Deere illustrate the value of using support to improve marketing effectiveness. Product support, however, is an underutilized marketing resource in many companies. Developing and executing support strategies with marketing impact is difficult, and managers frequently do not know where to begin.

To maximize the marketing impact, managers need to have an accurate idea of customer support expectations and how to measure them. They can then use this information to segment existing markets in a new way or, in some cases, even to define new markets.

In developing a support strategy, it is necessary for managers to make trade-offs between effectiveness and cost. Our studies show that these trade-offs are often quite complicated and need to be evaluated carefully. Managers need to understand the nature of each trade-off and to develop a suitable framework for choosing among competing alternatives.

Why support fails

To many people, product support means parts, service, and warranty. In the early stages of market growth, customers concentrate more on technology and features and are concerned with only a few aspects of support, such as parts and service. As the market starts to mature, customer needs become more sophisticated. Product support encompasses everything that can help maximize the customer's after-sales satisfaction—parts, service, and warranty plus operator training, maintenance training, parts delivery, reliability engineering, serviceability engineering, and even product design.

In many companies, however, the earlier limited view still holds sway; as a result they separate product support from marketing strategy. In our experience, companies in which this is the case exhibit some or all of the following characteristics:

An explicit support strategy is lacking. The company views product support as a collection of individual tasks—enhanced product and/or service reliability, upgraded parts availability, improved training of service personnel, investment in additional service facilities—without an overall integrating theme. Improving support means "more of the same."

Responsibility for support is diffused. Many companies do not centralize responsibility for product support; individual departments such as reliability engineering, service administration, and customer relations carry out support tasks. As a result, management receives a disjointed picture of product support and its relation both to the customers' needs and expectations and to the company's overall product design and marketing strategy.

Support needs are considered late in the development cycle. Managers often fail to contemplate such needs until after the design is frozen and the marketing strategy decisions have been made. Individual departments adopt support strategies that may not be compatible with one another.

Management focuses on individual support attributes. Because of the diffusion of responsibility, management tends to focus on internal matters—engineering reliability, parts availability, warranty costs—rather than on customer-oriented measures such as downtime per failure.

Taken together, the foregoing characteristics lead to an often-observed cycle:

1 Top management becomes concerned about customer complaints relating to product support.

2 Individual departments demand more resources to improve customer satisfaction.

3 Lacking an overall strategy, investments in individual areas (e.g., reliability, parts inventories) rapidly reach a point of diminishing returns.

4 Customer complaints continue because basic problems have not been addressed.

5 The cycle repeats.

The net result is a waste of resources and potential or actual loss of market share to competitors with superior support strategies. To break the cycle, managers must first appreciate how customer expectations can affect support and marketing strategies and then learn how to use these expectations constructively.

Segmenting the market

Customer expectations about product support add a crucial dimension to market segmentation. In most cases the package of support services that must be offered – implicitly or explicitly – changes significantly from one market segment to another. While many companies break down markets in terms of product features and performance, few segment markets on the basis of customers' support expectations. The result is that some support areas are overserviced while others are neglected.

Think of a word processor for a secretarial station. Potential buyers range from small one-secretary offices to large companies. There appear to be two market segments – one needing a basic model at a low price and the other a more comprehensive model at a higher price. Yet when customer expectations about support are analyzed, distinct differences emerge.

In the *one-machine office* the duration of downtime because of failure is crucial. Equipment failure means work virtually ceases, which can be extremely expensive. Disruption costs may be high because a small office cannot spare the people to search for replacements. The customer therefore expects both a low failure rate and minimum downtime per failure. Support costs or maintenance expenses are of secondary importance.

In the *multimachine office* downtime is important but not crucial; another functioning machine can be used to get important work out. Assuming that both the failure rate and downtime per failure are reasonably low, the customer is likely to be more interested in keeping maintenance and repair costs low over the life of the product.

These different expectations regarding support focus on varied attributes – failure frequency and downtime on the one hand, and maintenance and repair costs on the other – that form two distinct support segments. To meet customers' needs in each segment, management can choose a variety of strategies. For the word processor market, a company could (a) design for higher reliability (and charge a premium), (b) provide parts and service support as needed without a fixed-fee service contract, (c) develop a monthly service contract, or (d) use a spare machine on-site and incorporate its cost in the maintenance contract.

Each of these support strategies affects such major elements of marketing as product design and development, production and delivery, sales, and pricing. Choosing the right strategy involves a series of trade-offs such as product cost versus support effectiveness, product cost versus support cost, and support cost versus support effectiveness.

The importance of customer support expectations as an added dimension in market segmentation now becomes evident: different strategies are best for different segments. Ignoring these differences runs the risk of under- or overservicing segments, or under- or overpricing the product and the support services. The three steps involved in developing effective support strategies for a given product are:

1   Defining customer expectations regarding support.

2   Understanding the trade-offs implied in each support strategy.

3   Identifying the strategies that best fit management's objectives.

In planning a support program, however, managers need to be aware of the character of customer expectations, of the limitations of different support strategies, and of the interactions among strategies.

Defining customer needs

A major problem in segmenting the market on the basis of customer expectations lies in defining what these expectations are. Unlike product features or performance levels, customer support expectations focus on intangible attributes such as reliability, dependability, or availability. Without a suitable framework, the task of defining support segments is very difficult.

Because these intangible qualities can be viewed as proxies for underlying costs, the life-cycle cost concept used in equipment purchasing decisions can provide the basis for quantifying customer preferences regarding support. The life of a product after it is placed in service can be viewed as a sequence of uptimes and downtimes, terminated eventually by final failure, obsolescence, or sale and replacement. As the product goes through this cycle, customers can incur three types of costs:

1   Fixed costs on each failure occasion, independent of the length of downtime.

2   Variable costs that depend on the length of downtime and whose major component is the value of service lost (opportunity cost).

3   Maintenance costs of the product or service.

Because random events determine some of these costs, and since customers are likely to be risk averse, another factor must also be considered: uncertainty concerning the length and frequency of failure, the time needed for repair, and the magnitude of costs incurred.

To illustrate how underlying costs measure customer expectations, consider a washing machine used by a household and a large crawler tractor used by a builder. If the washing machine breaks, the homeowner incurs a repair bill (the fixed cost of failure). By and large, the homeowner is unwilling to pay a large premium to reduce the downtime (low variable costs of failure). Other things being equal, the purchaser of a domestic washing machine wants to keep repair costs low (high reliability).

On the other hand, if the crawler tractor breaks, the builder incurs significant fixed costs (of repair) and variable costs (wages paid to crews that sit idle until the tractor is back in action). Very often, the builder pays out more in wages for every hour the tractor is down than for repairs (the variable costs are far higher than the fixed costs). For this reason, the builder wants a tractor with both high reliability and low downtime per failure, and may even trade off reliability for less downtime.

In practice, customers incur fixed, variable, and maintenance costs. They are also risk averse and therefore concerned about uncertainty. Furthermore, as we have observed, in many cases customers do not clarify the relative importance of costs and risks. "I want a dependable product" often describes a wide variety of support needs. To define customer expectations accurately it is therefore necessary to find out which costs and risks customers are likely to be concerned about and then to develop suitable techniques for measuring them.

Measurable entities

Once the costs and risks of concern to the customer have been identified, managers can single out attributes such as reliability, availability, and dependability, and measure these in such terms as failure frequency, mean time between failures, downtime per failure, and the like.

While conceptually straightforward, translation of expectations into measurable terms is complicated by the fact that many customer expectations regarding support are nonlinear, support effectiveness is measured by many different variables, and statistical averages are misleading.

Nonlinear expectations

By and large, we are conditioned to think linearly: if one hour of downtime is bad, two hours are twice as bad. Unfortunately, customer expectations regarding support do not follow this simple logic. Instead, a threshold can be established for each expectation.

During the harvest season, for instance, farmers are extremely sensitive to the length of time a piece of farm equipment is out of commission because of a failure. Their reactions to downtimes lasting a half-day versus a day or more are vastly different. A downtime failure of a combine that can be repaired in four hours or less is tolerable; in fact, it often provides a welcome respite from harvesting. As the length of downtime increases past four to six hours, however, farmers become concerned, and by eight hours or so, they may be frantic. Beyond eight hours, the actual period of downtime is immaterial; farmers will go to almost any lengths to get up and running again – even if it means purchasing a new or used combine.

Farmers appear to have a similar threshold regarding the frequency with which a combine fails. Naturally, they hope it never fails; but, being realists, they're willing to accept an average of one or two failures per season. Farmers' tolerance of failure decreases very rapidly beyond this point, however, so that a combine design averaging three or four failures per season acquires a poor reputation. This attitude appears to be independent of the downtime duration at each failure; the number of failures is what the farmers remember, not how quickly the repairs were made.

Not all support expectations have clear thresholds. For instance, customers expect gradual improvements in the operational availability of a product or service (i.e., in its effective use during a given period). Since expected life-cycle costs – the purchase costs combined with discounted maintenance and repair costs less discounted salvage value, if any – vary in a smooth progression, expectations about these are predictable and linear. Customer reactions (to operational availability, life-cycle costs, and so on) are proportional to the value of the support variable.

Support effectiveness

Only in the case of low-cost household appliances like toasters or alarm clocks does a single variable such as reliability adequately measure support effectiveness. The farmer measures the support provided to his combine or tractor in terms of at least two variables – failure frequency and downtime per failure. The sophisticated purchaser of electronic office equipment weighs the support packages available as well as the training and programming assistance provided.

Moreover, customer preferences are often noncompensatory. Customers rank-order their preferences and do not consider an excess of one type of support as a substitute for deficiencies in another. A contractor buying a bulldozer, for example, wants both high reliability and low downtime per failure. He will be dissatisfied with any equipment that causes excessive downtime per failure, no matter how infrequently the failure occurs. Similarly, the office equipment buyer wants rapid response, irrespective of how infrequently it may be needed. For both, the risks and requirements of downtime are too high.

Statistical averages

One customer may get a dreamboat; another a lemon or a succession of lemons. Parts can be obtained over the counter – right away or ten days later. To cope with random fluctuations, people tend to use the average or the mean: the average weekly sales, the average wage rate, the average time between failures, and so forth.

In our investigations, we found ample evidence that averages are not only misleading but potentially dangerous when measuring support effectiveness. An industrial equipment company, for example, prided itself on the apparently high reliability of its product. Engineering tests indicated that the mean time between failures for its major product line was 400 hours. Since the average annual usage was 600 hours, management felt satisfied; after all, the machine experienced between one and two failures per year.

On conducting a survey of users, however, the company received a rude shock. True enough, the average number of failures was 1.65 per year. But, more than 40% of the users reported more than two failures a year; and of those, 20% had four or more failures. As the sales vice president put it, "If that's true, over 40% of our customers are not happy with our performance!"

This situation is also true of other support measures such as downtime per failure. These measures tend to be distributed in a skewed fashion, with a significant proportion of them lying well above the mean. For this reason, the mean is an extremely misleading measure. A more appropriate measure is a percentile, such as 80th or 90th percentile of the variable in question. This measure would have shown the industrial equipment company that a large proportion of their users were in fact experiencing more than two failures a year. Similarly, the office equipment company that assured purchasers, "We can usually have a service person out to your location within four to six hours" would have found that response time in the 80th percentile was closer to two working days.

Choosing an alternative

Having defined customer needs, the company can set about designing suitable support strategies. Normally, the manager can use one of several alternative support approaches. Each meets certain customer needs, such as greater reliability, shorter downtime per failure, or lower repair costs. At the same time, each affects the manufacturer's costs or revenues by creating higher product costs, increasing support costs, or lowering revenues. Choosing an alternative involves a trade-off between the effectiveness in meeting customer needs and impact on costs.

Such trade-offs are complex; neither effectiveness nor cost can be judged in terms of a single variable. Since support strategies meet diverse customer needs and affect the manufacturer's costs in various areas, trade-offs have to be made along several dimensions of effectiveness and cost.

Two additional factors further complicate the process of choosing a support strategy – the limitations of individual strategies and the interactions among strategies.

Limitations of strategies

The building blocks of any support package are the individual strategies designed to improve reliability, make the design modular, provide equipment on loan, and add diagnostic capabilities. *Exhibit I* lists some typical strategies, together with suppliers' costs and customers' benefits. While the impact of each varies with the technology and the industry, we have observed that all strategies exhibit diminishing returns to the customer, increasing costs to the supplier, and limited areas of impact.

Diminishing returns

Every support strategy produces diminishing returns with respect to customer benefits; beyond a certain point, further improvements are increasingly ineffective. For example, reliability improvements that extend the mean time between failures increase the availability of equipment to the customer, but the rate of increase slows down past a saturation point. Customers recognize this phenomenon, and once this point has been reached their focus shifts to other concerns, such as repair time.

Increasing costs

The initial improvements in any strategy are the simplest and therefore the cheapest. Succeeding improvements are progressively more expensive. It will cost the manufacturer more to raise the mean time between failures from 100 to 150 hours, for instance, than it did to raise it from 50 to 100 hours.

Limited impact

Each of the strategies shown in *Exhibit I* affects only part of the failure and restoration cycle. Diagnostics reduce the time required to locate the failure but do not affect repair time. Providing equipment on loan lowers the variable costs of a failure but does not alter the fixed costs.

Interactions of strategies

The foregoing limitations require the use of a suitable combination of individual strategies to meet customer needs. In synthesizing an overall strategy, a manager must know how individual strategies interact to ensure that the proposed combination achieves desired levels of customer benefits while keeping supplier costs as low as possible. Specifically, the manager needs to be aware of how strategy interactions can raise or lower overall costs to the supplier, complement benefits, and cause benefits substitution.

Cost adjustment

The way in which separate strategies interact affects the overall cost. For example, increasing reliability will lower the cost of supplying equipment on loan. It may, however, raise the cost of warranty repairs because it requires more expensive components.

Benefits complementarity

Certain combinations tend to reinforce the benefits of individual strategies. For instance, diagnostics are more effective with modular designs, which, in turn, are more effective when used in conjunction with on-site repair.

Benefits substitution

One strategy may serve as a substitute for another in terms of customer benefits. For example, speed of repair is less important when equipment loans are made available; therefore, both diagnostics and to a lesser degree modular design are substitutes for equipment on loan. Modular design reduces the need for large field inventories of spare parts; thus, these two strategies are to a certain extent substitutes for each other.

Exhibit I	Support strategies: costs and benefits		
Support strategy	**Suppliers' costs**	**Customers' benefits**
Improve product reliability	Design, engineering, and manufacturing	Lower rate of failure
Use modular designs, component exchange	Design, engineering, and inventory holding	Less downtime per failure, greater availability
Locate service facilities near markets	Site and facility; transportation and inventory	Faster access, less downtime, greater parts availability
Provide diagnostic equipment	Design, manufacturing, and service training	Faster diagnosis, less downtime, greater parts availability
Provide equipment on loan/standbys	Holding equipment for loan	Less downtime
Offer longer warranty periods and wider coverage	Warranty reserves and repair	Less uncertainty
Use mobile repair units	Transportation, inventory, and personnel	Faster response, improved service availability

Developing a structured process

The need to use several measures of cost and effectiveness and the limitations and interactions of individual strategies make a structured process for choosing support strategy essential. In its absence, a manager may not realize that existing strategies cost more and are less effective than alternatives, may yield to the pressures of individual departments and choose a suboptimal strategy, or may fail to make the decisions needed to stay competitive.

While situations vary, in general a manager should:

Define suitable measures of cost. Life-cycle costs are often appropriate; other measures can also be used.

Categorize all feasible support alternatives. Alternatives involving major design changes should not be excluded as they could be essential to improving support effectiveness.

Develop techniques to evaluate the cost and effectiveness of alternative strategies. Computer simulation, use of mathematical modeling, or field trials may be useful.

Measure the cost and effectiveness of each alternative. As measurements will be imprecise, it is necessary to show ranges and estimates of error.

Choose one measure of cost and another of effectiveness and plot the results. The most important or significant measures should be analyzed in this step; other measures will be checked later.

Identify key strategies. Some strategies will stand out as superior in cost and effectiveness.

Repeat trade-off analysis using other measures. Determining if different measures change key strategies is a valuable check.

This process can narrow the options to two or three major choices. The final decision will depend on external factors such as management's preferences, the competitive situation, or other marketing or product concerns.

What to focus on

Support strategies are not static; a strategy that is effective today will, if unchangeable, become ineffective in meeting future customer needs. Generally, customer satisfaction increases with improvements in one area (e.g., reliability) up to a point. As diminishing returns to the customer set in and the manufacturer's costs increase, companies will need to switch to another, often radically different strategy, like lending equipment. And when customers demand higher levels of satisfaction than can be economically provided with loaners, the company has to switch to still another approach, like improving access to components that fail and thereby reducing repair time.

This pattern appears to be characteristic of product support systems in general. A different, dominant strategy provides the most customer satisfaction at successive stages, and the level of customer satisfaction increases progressively. Each rise in the level of satisfaction raises the manufacturer's costs and accentuates the need for choosing another, more efficient support strategy.

To ensure that their products remain competitive, managers must identify the various stages that exist for their products and market segments. Having chosen a support strategy, they must ascertain their company's and competitors' relative positions, anticipate when customer needs or competitive pressures will require the company to shift to the next stage, and plan for shifts in support strategy.

A manufacturer's relative market position often determines support strategy. If customers

Exhibit II	Alternative support strategies for an industrial tractor
Key	**Strategy**
A	Improve fill rate for parts from 91% to 95%
B	Improve mean time between failures from 350 to 450 hours
C	Develop and install microprocessor-based diagnostic capability in each tractor
D	Provide faster parts service using parts vans
E	Redesign tractor to permit faster modular exchange of electrical and hydraulic components
F	Provide users with tractors on loan during serious failures
G	Redesign tractor for modular exchange of electrical, hydraulic, and engine-driven train components
H	Redesign tractor as in strategy E and provide loaners
I	Redesign tractor as in strategy G and provide loaners
J	Redesign tractor as in strategy C; provide loaners and built-in diagnostics

and competitors perceive the company as a leader in identifying and meeting support needs, management can set the pace at which support effectiveness is improved. On the other hand, a company that is perceived as an "also ran" has to follow and, if possible, anticipate changes in the strategies of any leaders or in customer expectations.

Since shifting to a new stage raises the level of effectiveness considerably, companies that are slow to react to changes in customer needs and/or the level of support provided by competitors risk being frozen out. Improvements in the level of support given in other industries, raising customers' expectations across the board; pressure on competitors to maintain or increase market share; and introduction of new support techniques—any or all of these could signal the need for a shift. Managers also need to plan for such shifts to ensure that existing support strategies don't box them in.

Designing support: a case study

An industrial equipment manufacturer started to design a new series of industrial tractors to replace its current models in the mid- to late-1980s. The company was aware of customer dissatisfaction regarding existing levels of support, which it had made several efforts to improve. Realizing the

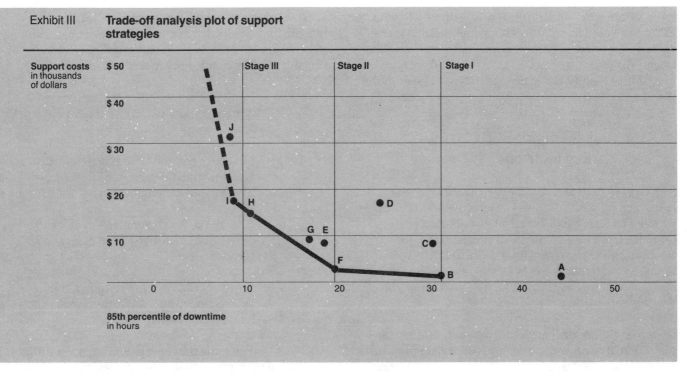

Exhibit III   **Trade-off analysis plot of support strategies**

value of designing support and product strategies in parallel and recognizing that responsibility for support was fragmented, management appointed a study team reporting to the president. The team's charter was to develop strategies that would profitably deliver superior support for the new series of industrial tractors.

Existing marketing data indicated a number of diverse customer needs regarding product support. Although it identified individual support elements such as greater parts availability, higher reliability, and more service training, the data gave little insight as to how customers measured overall support effectiveness or made purchase decisions.

To determine failure frequency, causes of failure, downtime per failure, and the components of downtime, the study team mailed a survey to the entire user population and received more than 3,000 responses. In addition, the team used a combination of focus groups and in-field interviews to determine customer preferences and develop measures of support effectiveness.

The team's investigations showed that customers focused on two key factors: the downtime caused by an individual tractor failure and a combination of how often their tractors failed, how much total downtime these failures caused, and the level of regular maintenance required.

The relative importance of these factors in purchase decisions varied. For one customer group, downtime per failure made the greatest impact on purchase decisions, while a second group weighed other factors as well. This suggested the existence of two separate support segments. The team decided to use

the following measures of support effectiveness for both segments: the 85th percentile of downtime per failure (i.e., no more than 15% of the failures exceed this level of downtime), and the annual operational availability or ratio of uptime to the sum of uptime, downtime, and maintenance time.

The team felt that the operational availability ratio best captured the effects of improvements in engineering reliability. It also smoothed out random fluctuations in parts availability and showed the impact of improvements in maintainability and serviceability.

When the team analyzed the causes of downtime, it found that parts delay accounted for more than half the total downtime, with repair time taking up a third, and travel time the rest. This fact suggested some alternative strategies: increased dealer-level parts inventories, improved service training, and the use of mobile repair vans. Where downtime was critical, equipment on loan would be furnished, if economical.

When the team analyzed the causes of failures, it discovered that a large number were breakdowns in electrical and hydraulic components. Individually, these failures were easy to repair; their cumulative effect was, however, large. Engine and power-train failures did not have the same impact because, while each failure caused considerable downtime, such failures occurred infrequently. These facts suggested some additional strategies: improved reliability (especially of electrical and hydraulic components) and tractor design to permit modular exchange of defective components in the field.

After identifying all feasible alternatives, summarized in *Exhibit II*, the team developed a computer-based simulator, which duplicated as far as possible the effect of using a given strategy or combination of strategies in terms of downtime and operational availability. Finally, the team calculated the costs of the various alternatives, using a life-cycle cost model.

Key trade-offs

To identify the optimal choices, the team then plotted the costs and effectiveness of the various strategies. *Exhibit III* shows a typical plot. Overall, effectiveness improved substantially (for example, the 85th percentile of downtime was reduced from 45 hours to 10 hours or less. However, support costs increased at least fourfold too). In addition, the analysis showed that:

☐ While parts delay was a significant factor in total downtime, improving parts availability had little impact. This was because most repairs required several parts, and absence of even one part caused at least a one-day delay because of shipping time.
☐ Built-in diagnostics had little impact; in most cases, diagnostic time wasn't important.
☐ Equipment on loan was not economic until overall reliability had reached approximately 400 hours between failures.
☐ Equipment loans and modular exchange were complementary. Loaners reduced customer downtime while modular exchange reduced the number of loaners by allowing rapid in-field repairs.

As shown in *Exhibit III*, there were basically three stages—from 50 hours of downtime to 30 hours, from 30 hours to 20 hours, and from 20 hours to 10 hours. In each stage, the most efficient strategy was quite different. In Stage I, improving reliability was the best strategy. In Stage II, providing loaners was the most efficient, while in Stage III, a combination of modular exchange and loaners was most efficient.

Management's choices

After reviewing the team's analysis, management decided that under current market conditions, supplying loaners (Strategy F in *Exhibit II*) was the most cost-effective. However, loaners would not provide long-term advantages because competitors could easily do the same. Therefore, the company decided to make major changes in its design philosophy and to aim for greater modularization of critical components. A combination of modular exchange and loaners would provide superior support at least cost, while the long lead times required for design changes would ensure long-term competitive advantage. Management therefore decided to proceed as follows:

1 Improve the reliability of its existing design to allow use of equipment on loan.

2 Introduce equipment on loan (Strategy F) in the mid-1980s, or earlier if competitive pressures demanded it.

3 Change its design approach to allow progressive modularization of key components.

4 Switch over to a combination of modular exchange and loans (Strategies H and I) in the late 1980s.

The industrial equipment manufacturer needed three to five years to change its design and to modularize its components. Had the company concentrated on improving reliability of its existing product, it would have found itself locked in and unable to change without incurring large engineering and tooling costs as well as a premature phase-out of its current designs. ⊟

Reprint 83611

READ THE FINE PRINT

REPRINTS
Telephone: 617-495-6192
Fax: 617-495-6985

Current and past articles are available, as is an annually updated index. Discounts apply to large-quantity purchases.

Please send orders to
HBR Reprints
Harvard Business School
Publishing Division
Boston, MA 02163.

HOW CAN *HARVARD BUSINESS REVIEW* ARTICLES WORK FOR YOU?

For years, we've printed a microscopically small notice on the editorial credits page of the *Harvard Business Review* alerting our readers to the availability of *HBR* articles.

Now we invite you to take a closer look at some of the many ways you can put this hard-working business tool to work for you.

IN THE CORPORATE CLASSROOM.

There's no more effective, or cost-effective, way to supplement your corporate training programs than in-depth, incisive *HBR* articles.

Affordable and accessible, it's no wonder hundreds of companies and consulting organizations use *HBR* articles as a centerpiece for management training.

IN-BOX INNOVATION.

Where do your company's movers and shakers get their big ideas? Many find the inspiration for innovation in the pages of *HBR*. They then share the wealth and spread the word by distributing *HBR* articles to company colleagues.

IN MARKETING AND SALES SUPPORT.

HBR articles are a substantive leave-behind to your sales calls. And they can add credibility to your direct mail campaigns. They demonstrate that your company is on the leading edge of business thinking.

CREATE CUSTOM ARTICLES.

If you want to pack even greater power in your punch, personalize *HBR* articles with your company's name or logo. And get the added benefit of putting your organization's name before your customers.

AND THERE ARE 500 MORE REASONS IN THE *HBR CATALOG*.

In all, the *Harvard Business Review Catalog* lists articles on over 500 different subjects. Plus, you'll find books and videos on subjects you need to know.

The catalog is yours for just $8.00. To order *HBR* articles or the *HBR Catalog* (No. 21019), call 617-495-6192. Please mention telephone order code 025A when placing your order. Or FAX us at 617-495-6985.

And start putting *HBR* articles to work for you.

**Harvard Business School
Publications**

Call 617-495-6192 to order the *HBR Catalog*.

(Prices and terms subject to change.)

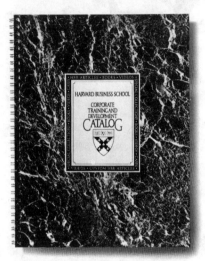